RAVE REVIEWS FOR *EVITA—FIRST LADY*

DALLAS MORNING NEWS:

"A fabulous biography."

LOS ANGELES HERALD EXAMINER:

"Barnes' biography is brisk, pointed and thoroughly fascinating."

MIAMI HERALD:

"John Barnes' excellent book is a splendid evocation of the woman and her times—the most precious ingredient of any creditable biography."

ARIZONA REPUBLIC:

"Fascinating!"

HOUSTON POST:

"Marvelous.... A story that moves faster and faster as it ticks off the 33 years of this amazing woman."

ORLANDO STAR SENTINEL:

"A fascinating and readable account.... Any list of the most influential women of the 20th century would have to include Eva Peron."

CHICAGO SUN-TIMES:

"John Barnes describes her life with a veteran storyteller's robust style, rich in fascinating detail and confidential anecdote."

NASHVILLE BANNER:

"John Barnes has recognized both the good and the bad of Evita. He tells why she was loved—and hated by so many. Eva Peron was one of the most important figures in modern history. Important enough to be a legend."

AMERICAN LIBRARY ASSOCIATION BOOKLIST:

"Evita is here the subject of a balanced, sober portrait. Barnes appreciates the passion Evita stirred as she clawed her way to power: her rags to riches life...."

NEWARK STAR-LEDGER:

"Barnes has made an exciting book out of an exciting story."

CHARLESTON EVENING POST:

"A colorful account of one of the most powerful women in history."

TIME:

"The mystique continues...greed, hate and passion too real to dismiss."

EVITA
FIRST LADY
A Biography of Eva Perón

John Barnes

GROVE PRESS, INC./NEW YORK

First Black Cat Edition 1979
Fifth Printing 1981
ISBN: 0-394-17087-3
Grove Press ISBN: 0-8021-4256-7
Library of Congress Catalog Card Number: 78-3185

Library of Congress Cataloging in Publication Data

Barnes, John, 1935-
  Evita, First Lady.

  Includes index.
  1. Perón, Eva Duarte, 1919-1952. 2. Argentine Republic — Presidents — Wives — Biography. 3. Women in politics — Argentine Republic — Biography.
I. Title.
F2849.P37B3   982′.06′0924 [B]   78-3185
ISBN: 0-394-17087-3

Manufactured in the United States of America

Distributed by Random House, Inc., New York

GROVE PRESS, INC., 196 West Houston Street, New York, N.Y. 10014

GROVE PRESS, INC., 196 West Houston Street, New York, N.Y. 10014

· CONTENTS ·

ILLUSTRATIONS

The start of a formal evening
A gala night
Evita held up by her husband
A warm embrace
Between pages 168 and 169
Voting for her husband
The last public appearance
Queueing to view the body
Crazed with grief
The flowers
Evita's Milan grave
Juan and Evita united
The Duarte tomb
In life and death

PROLOGUE

*Estas cosas pense en la Recoleta
en el lugar de mi ceniza.*

These thoughts came to me in the Recoleta
in the place where my ashes will lie.

Jorge Luis Borges

In the early hours of October 22, 1976, an Argentine army truck loaded with well-armed troops drove out through the gates of the presidential residence in Olivos and headed towards Buenos Aires, a few miles away. It was followed by an ambulance, which in turn was followed by another truck. The convoy drove through the still dark streets of the capital to Recoleta Cemetery, a little city of the dead where the bodies of presidents, generals, and other illustrious Argentines are housed in rows of opulent, mansion-sized vaults along avenues lined with cyprus trees. It is *the* place to be buried in Argentina, the most fashionable necropolis in a country where the dead, like the living, are judged by their houses. Thirteen of the country's presidents are there. So is Luis Angel Firpo, the Wild Bull of the Pampas, who earned his place in the national pantheon with a punch that knocked Jack Dempsey out of the ring, although Dempsey climbed back in to beat him. Outside his vault stands a bigger than life size bronze statue of the 'Bull' in his dressing gown and fighting boots. Around him, in the cemetery's bleak, grassless chaos of marble and granite, soaring spires and domes cast shadows on generals on horseback and politicians exhorting invisible crowds. Bronze scrolls on the vaults list the inhabitants' honours. Inside, ornate coffins are draped with lace, lined with candles, and decorated with flowers. There are chairs for living visitors. Circular stairways wind down into the earth where other family members are buried. The place is full. There's an Argentine saying: 'It's easier to get into heaven than into Recoleta.'

Understandably, it is one of the most popular attractions in Argentina. More than a thousand people stroll down Recoleta's cold streets every day — not only the old women, the regulars at every cemetery with their bunches of fresh flowers, but also the tourist groups from the provinces with cameras and school children in white smocks on their class outing stare at the houses of the famous dead.

But there were no visitors on that chill morning of October 22. It was too early for the old women, and, anyway, the cemetery was ringed by policemen carrying sub-machine guns to deter the curious as the convoy of army trucks and ambulance ground to a halt outside the doric portico of Recoleta's front entrance. Two cemetery workers, called in for special duty, helped unload a coffin that was covered by a mattress so that no one, not even the soldiers, could take a peak at the face of the woman who lay serenely beneath the glass top. Surrounded by their military guard, the workers carried the coffin along one of the avenues, then down a narrow side street, stopping in front of a black marble crypt belonging to the 'Familia Duarte'. They carried it inside. There was no ceremony. The workmen removed the mattress and quickly left, slamming the ornate steel gate locked behind them. 'The soldiers were nervous and in a hurry,' said one of the workers later. 'They just wanted to plant her and get out of there.'

The nervousness of the soldiers was understandable. They had just 'planted' Eva Perón, the long dead wife of former President Juan Perón and the beloved Saint Evita of millions of adoring Argentines. It was the second time in almost quarter of a century that the military, who so often rule Argentina, had hurriedly disposed of Eva's body in a desperate effort to purge their country of the turbulent passions inspired by her name.

During her lifetime, at the height of her career in the late 1940s, Maria Eva Duarte de Perón was one of the most loved and hated, powerful and capricious women in Argentina and the world.

When she died in 1952, her widower, President Perón, was never able to persuade his people that he was now the substance and she the shadow. Within three years, Perón had been overthrown, fleeing into exile aboard a Paraguayan gunboat. Argentina's long-repressed anti-Perónists erased every physical vestige of Evita. Bulldozers tore down her monuments. Her pictures, books, personal papers were burned in public bonfires. Even her body disappeared from the Confederation of Labour headquarters where it had been kept to await the completion of a multi-million dollar mausoleum, which was to be taller than the Statue of Liberty.

For sixteen years the body of Evita Perón was missing. But in Argentina, the cult of Saint Evita flourished, dooming every attempt by the nation's generals to return the government to stable civilian rule. Posters of an ethereal Evita plastered the walls of every town and village in the country. Terrorists killed in her name. The president who had taken power soon after Juan Perón was overthrown was kidnapped and murdered in an unsuccessful effort to make him tell where Evita's body had been hidden. Finally, however, the Argentine Army capitulated. In Lot 86, Garden 41 in Musocco Cemetery in Milan, Italy, the body of Maria Maggi, an Italian woman who had died in Argentina, was exhumed. The coffin's wooden casing was rotting. But the coffin itself, of silver with a glass window, was in excellent condition. So was the corpse. It was the embalmed body of Evita Perón.

Over two decades, she travelled far and wide — a macabre odyssey across five countries of two continents. Now that she has been interred in Argentine soil, perhaps her fellow countrymen will let her rest in peace. But it is doubtful. There is a macabre, almost necrophiliac love of the dead in the soul of the Argentine people. Famous cadavers have often stood for national causes in the years since the country won its independence from Spain in 1810. It is as if the body had become the flag of political battle. Possession is everything, in a way it is like owning a splinter of the True Cross. There is also the terror of it falling into the hands of the enemy — the fear of defilement. In the early days of the nation when a provincial *caudillo* (dictator), General Juan la Valle, was shot dead by his enemies, his friends dug up the body and carried it on horseback out of the country to Bolivia for safe-keeping. When it began to decompose on the trail, the funeral escort dismounted, skinned and eviscerated the corpse and carried on, packing the relics in saddlebags. Even today, the battle over the bones of another nineteenth-century dictator continues as fiercely as ever. Posters plastered on city walls proclaim that 'Rosas Lives'. But, in fact, Juan Manuel de Rosas, a fierce, throat-cutting *gaucho* (cowboy) has been dead for over a hundred years. He created the first secret police in South America and ruthlessly forged the country's quarrelling provinces into a single nation before he was overthrown. He lived out his remaining years in Southampton, where he is buried. But in Argentina, the question of whether his bones should be brought back to his homeland still provokes controversy among pro- and anti-Rosas factions.

But Argentina is not just a land in love with the heroic dead. Grotesque death in every conceivable form is a ritualistic everyday business in Argentina, where left-wing guerrillas kidnap, torture, and murder, and, in turn, are themselves captured, tortured, and then often taken out of their cells and machine-gunned or dynamited together in bundled groups. Perhaps it is something in the character of the people who inhabit this remote, empty, desolate land of a million square miles — five times the size of France — a brutish land of plunder, virtually peopled in this century. In 1850, there were fewer than a million Argentines, and Indian territory began less than a hundred miles from Buenos Aires. Those Argentines were the descendants of the hardy soldier-adventurers of Spain who first colonised the land in the early 1500s. They became the gauchos, the cowboys who pushed out into the vast Indian-infested grazing lands called the pampas, rolling plains which stretch from the sweltering jungles of the Chaco on the Bolivian border in the north to the freezing antarctic wastes of Patagonia in the south, from the snow-capped Andes in the west to the Atlantic in the east.

'It was the gaucho who made Argentina,' wrote John White in his *Life Story of a Nation*. 'First, he helped the Spaniards win the country from the Indians by providing an effective barrier between the civilised towns and the raiding savages. Later, he formed the mounted militias which won freedom from Spain, not only for Argentina but for Uruguay, Chile, Bolivia and Peru. Then, after many years of civil war, he finally forced the

City and Province of Buenos Aires to join the Federation. It was then, and not until then, that Argentina became a nation.' So the gaucho is the national hero of Argentina, immortalised in a long epic poem, *El Gaucho Martin Fierro*. Most Argentines can recite a few verses of the poem in which the gaucho extols liberty, manhood, and justice. But Walter Owen, *Martin Fierro's* English translator, took a clearer-eyed view of the gaucho in his introduction, one that could just as easily apply in many ways to the present day Argentine.

He was, wrote Owen, a 'strange mixture of virtues and vices, of culture and savagery. Arrogant and self-respecting, religious, punctilious within the limits of his own peculiar code, he was yet patient under injustice, easily led and impressed by authority, ferocious, callous, brutal, superstitious and improvident.' He was as 'pitiless as the savage Guaycurus (Indians) of his native plains, who as an old chronicler says, were "the most turbulent of heathen, who extract their eyelashes to better see the Christians and slay them." . . . In no country and at no time, perhaps, has a race existed among which physical courage, intrepidity, indifference to suffering and endurance have been held in such high esteem.' The gaucho's law was his knife, or *facon*, a short sword with a double-edged curved blade. His poncho wrapped around his left arm and used as a shield, he fought, whirling his facon, waiting for an opportunity for a sweeping blow that would lay his opponent's throat open. To the gaucho, throat-cutting was the only satisfactory way of killing an enemy. W. H. Hudson, the English naturalist and novelist who was born and grew up in Argentina in the middle of the 1800s recollected in his book *Far Away and Long Ago* listening as a child to groups of gauchos as they sat around and yarned at the close of day in the *pulperia*, the village store, bar, and general meeting place.

Inevitably, the talk turned sooner or later to the subject of cutting throats. Not to waste powder on prisoners was an unwritten law and the veteran gaucho clever with the knife took delight in obeying it. Remembered Hudson: 'It always came as a relief, I heard them say, to have as a victim a young man with a good neck after an experience of tough, scraggy old throats: with a person of that sort they were in no hurry to finish the business; it was performed in a leisurely, loving way . . . He did his business rather like a hellish creature revelling in his cruelty. He would listen to all his captive could say to soften his heart — all his heartrending prayers and pleadings; and would reply:

"ah, friend," or little friend, or brother — "your words pierce me to the heart and I would gladly spare you for the sake of that poor mother of yours who fed you with her milk, and for your own sake too, since in this short time I have conceived a great friendship towards you; but your beautiful neck is your undoing, for how could I possibly deny myself the pleasure of cutting such a throat — so shapely, so smooth and soft and so white! Think of the sight of warm red blood gushing from that white column!" And so on, with wavings of the steel blade before the captive's eyes, until the end.'

It was a cruel, brutal country out there on the plains in no-man's land beyond the frontier posts of the Argentine army. For the settlers, pushing west and south in their bullock-wagons, the greatest terror was reserved for the Indians, who bitterly resisted the encroachment on their ancestral hunting grounds. Even the tough gaucho felt a fear and respect for them. It was a similar story of course on the North American plains, thousands of miles away. In both countries, encroaching white settlers viewed the embattled Indians as savage beasts—

'Those horrible howling bands,' wrote the gaucho Martin Fierro

That fall like a swarm on town and farm;
Before the Christian has time to arm,
They have seen the sign; they have sniffed the wind
And they come like the desert sand . . .

The only thing in his savage creed
That the Indian's sure about
Is this: that it's always good to kill,
And of smoking blood to drink his fill:
And the blood he can't drink when his belly's full
He likes to see bubble out . . .

Like ravening beasts on the scent of blood
They come o'er the desert broad,
Their terrible cries fill the earth and skies
And make every hair on your head to rise,
Every mother's son of their howling horde
Seems a devil damned by God.

In 1832, when Rosas was busy trying to wipe out the pampas Indians, his camp was visited by Charles Darwin during the British naturalist's historic voyage in HMS *Beagle* to Latin

America. Darwin described the place as looking more like the hide-out of brigands than the headquarters of a nation's army. Guns, wagons and crude straw huts had been formed into a sort of compound, 400 yards square. Encamped within it were the general's gauchos. The young Englishman was fascinated by them — their mustachios, long black hair falling down over their shoulders, their scarlet ponchos and wide riding trousers, white boots with huge spurs, and knives stuck in their waistbands. They were extremely polite and looked, Darwin said, 'as if they would cut your throat and make a bow at the same time.' He got the same feeling about their general — extremely courteous but capable of ordering a man to be shot on the slightest whim.

Rosas's campaign strategy against the Indians was simple. He rounded them up a hundred or so at a time and slaughtered them without compunction or mercy — men, women and children. In fact, while Darwin was in the camp, a company of gauchos rode off on an Indian hunt. They spotted a party of Indians crossing the open plain, and after killing a few who fought when cornered, they finally rounded up 110 men, women, and children. They shot all the men except three who they kept for interrogation. The better looking girls were set aside to be distributed among the gauchos. But the older women and the uglier girls were also killed immediately. The children were kept to be sold as slaves. The three surviving Indians were then shot in turn as they refused to divulge the whereabouts of the rest of the tribe, the third of them pushing out his chest proudly as he told his captors, 'Fire, I am a man. I can die.'

To the horrified Darwin, it was the Argentines who were the savages, not the Indians. But then he was a genteel young man from the peaceful Shropshire countryside. While his voyage led him to a revolutionary concept of the evolution of life, he was incapable of understanding the basic facts of life in a raw, brutal land. It was win or die. Prisoners always had their throats cut after battle. It came as no surprise to them. As for the charming Rosas, he ruled through terror and repression. He allowed no constitution or parliament. He banned books and newspapers. But he enjoyed wide support among the people who counted for nothing in Argentina — the poor, the gauchos, who worshipped him. He could throw the bolas, break horses, and cut throats with the best of them.

He once explained to a friend how he held on to power. Although he was a landowner, he said, he knew and understood the lower classes. 'I know and respect the talents of many of the men who have governed the country . . . But it seems to me that all committed a great error; they governed very well for the cultured people but scorned the lower classes, the people of the fields, who were the men of action. I believe it is important to establish a major influence over this class to contain it and direct it, and I have acquired this influence. I am a gaucho among gauchos. I talk as they do. I protect them. I am their attorney. I care for their interests.'

The Indians of the Argentine plains were doomed by the hatred and terror they inspired. For a large part of the last century they held back the white tide with their raids on isolated farms and military outposts, armed with nothing more than their eighteen-foot lances tipped with a foot-long blade, their *bolas*, three heavy metal balls attached to ropes which were whirled and thrown to upend their enemies, and their bows and arrows. But eventually — and less than one hundred years ago — the Argentine cavalry swept through the pampas. Unlike the United States, where the Indian survivors were rounded up and herded into reservations, in Argentina the slaughter was total. Indian settlements were razed to the ground. The few remnants of a proud and skilled people were sent to Buenos Aires as captive servants. Even rebellious gauchos, known as *montoneros*, who on more than one occasion had taken on the national army in open battle, were exterminated or brought to heel. The vast lands of the pampas, ripe for exploitation, disappeared into the hands of generals, the land-owning aristocrats of colonial descent, and speculators. British-built railways probed out into the empty land, carrying hundreds of thousands of Spanish and Italian immigrants to work as peasants on the land, living in mud and straw huts, transient hovels for men who felt no kinship to the rich, black pampas soil but dreamed of earning enough from it to take back to the land of their birth.

Not even the *estancieros*, the wealthy ranchers who owned hundreds of thousands of pampas acres — estates as large as English counties — sank any roots in this desolate, monotonous land. To them it was a commodity. The railways carried their grain and cattle to the port city of Buenos Aires. From there the wheat and meat were shipped on to the booming markets in Europe. Overnight, the cattle ranchers from Argentina became the world's newest nouveau riche. They owned mansions in Buenos Aires, Paris, and London. On their lands in the pampas

8

they built French chateaux and gabled English country homes, surrounded with eucalyptus groves, lawns and rose gardens, which they visited on the occasional weekend. But the wealth of the land was such that it could support those who milked it with such abandon (there is an old Argentine saying which has stood the test of time — no matter how hard Argentines try they can never bankrupt Argentina).

The land could also support the thousands of immigrants pouring into the port of Buenos Aires every week. They came in such numbers that the population soared from nearly 2 million in 1869 to 4 million in 1895 and 8 million in 1914. By then three out of every four adults in Buenos Aires were European born. The vast majority of the nation possessed no ties that bound them together as one people with a feeling and understanding for one another — outside the family the lack of tolerance of Argentines towards one another has haunted the nation down to this day. At the turn of the century, at the critical moment of nation-building, the only bond among the thousands of new Argentines pouring into Buenos Aires was that in building a new city in place of the old-fashioned, large village (la grand aldea) between the River Plate and the pampas, they, as labourers on the building sites, in the cattle slaughter houses, and on the dockside, and the carpenters, grocers, milkmen, butchers, servants, householders, and peddlers, all owed their livelihood to the vast, empty hinterland beyond the city.

It was a land, wrote American poet Archibald MacLeish, 'in which the distances from house to house are too great for the barking of dogs on the stillest night; a country in which the cock crows only twice because there is no answer . . . a country so level that even time has no hold on it and one century is like another; a country so empty that the watches at night put their eyes along the ground to see the circle of the horizon; a country in which the sky is so huge that men plant islands of eucalyptus trees over the houses to be covered from the blue. It is a country of grass, a country without stone, a country in which the women are always together under the dark trees in the evening, their faces fading into the loneliness with the night.'

It was on the pampas, near the village of Los Toldos in the Province of Buenos Aires, some 150 miles west of the Argentine capital, that Maria Eva Ibarguren was born on May 7, 1919, in a ramshackle farmhouse built of mud bricks and roofed with tiles of red clay and corrugated iron.

1

THE WRONG SIDE OF THE TRACKS

'If ever a man wishes to know what it is to have an inclination to commit suicide, let him spend a week in a rural town in Argentina.'

It was a foreign visitor to the Argentine pampas who made that remark long ago in the 1890s. Los Toldos is that kind of town. It hadn't changed from the days when it was a frontier outpost less than fifty years before Eva Ibarguren was born. It's still the same today — a dreary, squalid, little *pueblo,* built on the site of a long-forgotten Indian encampment. Dusty, unpaved streets wander out from the grassless, empty plaza and disappear into the plains. Dust covers everything, a foot thick on the ground, choking up in yellow clouds with the passing of each truck or herd of cattle, colouring the brown mud walls of the houses a faded grey. When the violent south-west wind, the *pampero,* blows across the pampas, Los Toldos disappears from view in the dust. Then black clouds sweep out from the horizon, swallowing up the sky, unleashing thunder, lightning and torrents of rain, isolating the pueblo in a sea of mud.

Juana Ibarguren, a pretty, plump girl of Basque descent, lived on the edge of the town. It was not much of a home; one room and a patio shared with the chickens, goats, and five children. But then her lover, Juan Duarte, a local landowner, already had a wife and other children to support in Chivilcoy, another rather larger pampas town not far away. Still, he was a man of moderate means and it was naturally accepted that he would have another woman elsewhere. In fact, he would have been thought of as odd by his friends if he had not. *Machismo* — the cult of sexual conquest — was, still is, deeply rooted in the Argentine way of life. Women, legally as well as socially, were regarded as part of a man's material possessions, as wives, virgin daughters, and mistresses — the first two to be protected from dishonour, the third to be pursued and used for pleasure. A wife could not get a divorce in Argentina (she still cannot) and, legally, both she and her children were considered part of her husband's property. She expected him to be unfaithful. She might not like it. But she put up with it as long as he did not embarrass her by flaunting his girl friend in their own social strata. In wealthy families, he would have his *garçonnière*, bachelor rooms, in a discreet block of flats in town. For those who could not afford such luxuries, there were always the *amoblados*, love hotels which exist in every town and city in Argentina, where rooms are rented by the hour. In the countryside, in the home of the wealthy estancieros, the sons of the family gained their sexual experience with the servant girls or the daughters of the estancia's farmworkers. They could not, of course, sleep with a girl from their own class of society. Her virginity was the most prized family possession of all, to be relinquished only for the price of a good marriage.

For the poor girl on the pampas, virginity was almost certainly a thing of the past by her fourteenth birthday. Few could expect anything more from life than grinding poverty. However, if she was really pretty, there was always the possibility that she might find a married man of means to support her. Juana Ibarguren was certainly pretty in a plump, pinchable sort of way. She also had an effervescent personality, the kind that usually gets what it wants. At the Duarte farm in Chivilcoy, where she worked as a cook, she had quickly fastened her flashing dark eyes on the master of the house. It was not long before she was pregnant with the first of her five children, all of them born in the one-room house that Juan Duarte had rented for her in in her home town. Her father had been the local coachman in Los Toldos, carrying the rich estancia families in his horse and trap to and from the local railway station, where Juana's brother worked as the stationmaster. So she was not from the very lowest rung of rural peasant life, which often dispensed with the cost and formality of marriage. Perhaps then, it was understandable that some of her more 'respectable' neighbours looked with disapproval at Juana Ibarguren and her growing number of illegitimate children.

But her relationship with Juan Duarte was a stable one. After all, it lasted for nearly fifteen years. Even if he did not live with the family, Juan visited them frequently. But although they were not deprived of his love and affection, they learnt at a very early age what it was like to be branded as bastards. Los Toldos was so small it could hardly be called a town, just a stop on the little railway line that meanders for a 100 miles through that part of the pampas, giving up midway to the next village of O'Brien.

Everyone led much the same squalid, poverty-stricken life. Even so, the Ibarguren children were ostracised. Neighbours would not let their own children play with them. But while that is something that no child would ever forget, the deepest scarring experience in Eva's childhood — she was the youngest and nearly seven at the time — occurred when her father died. Juana Ibarguren, being a practical woman, knew that she could not go to the funeral (which in Argentina has to take place within 24 hours of death) because of the bitter hatred that Juan Duarte's wife, Estela Grisolia, felt for her. But she wanted her children to see their father for the last time. So the girls — Elisa, the eldest, who was about 16, Blanca 14, and Arminda, a year older than Eva — were dressed in mourning, black smocks and long black stockings, while Juan, the 10-year-old boy, wore a band of crepe around his sleeve. They set out on their first ever ride in a sulky to the Duarte estancia. But when they got there, they were not allowed into the house.

With death and funerals occupying such significant roles in Argentine life, Dona Estela was determined not to allow the evidence of her late husband's unfaithfulness to be displayed in public around his coffin. So the bewildered little girls and their brother sat up in the sulky, crying their eyes out, not really comprehending what it was all about. Finally, a brother of the dead man interceded on behalf of 'those little wretches who want to take one last look'. They were allowed to follow the coffin, in Indian file, after the family to the local cemetery.

Life was rough for Juana Ibarguren for the next couple of years. Juan Duarte had been her sole means of support. All that he left her was a legal declaration that her children were his — in order for them to be able to bear his name. So, in order to pay the rent

13

for her tiny one-room house, she and the girls hired themselves out as cooks in the homes of the local estancias. It was then that Eva got her first close look at the rich, powerful families who controlled Argentina through the wealth generated by their ownership of the land. In Buenos Aires Province, which includes Los Toldos and is the largest of the pampas provinces, 15 families owned a million acres of land each. Another 50 families owned 50,000 acres. The estancias where Eva often worked existed virtually as independent mini-kingdoms. They had their own schools, chapels and hospitals. The estanciero families would divide their year between Paris and Buenos Aires, visiting the estancia usually at Christmas-time, at the start of the long, hot Argentine summer. Their journey to and from their nearest pampas railway station was, more often that not, their only connection with the tiny pueblos that had grown up around the stations that the British-owned railways had built to serve the estancias. For Eva, helping out in the kitchens, it was a world to be gawked at as a child — the crowds of guests and children, the nannies, governesses and major domos, and the patron, wearing the inevitable, expensive imitation of the clothes that the impoverished gauchos wore on the plains.

Eva never forgot those years or the dusty, grubby little pueblo by the railways tracks. In her autobiography, *La Razon de mi Vida* (The Reason for my Life), published shortly before she died in 1952, she recalled her childhood: 'I remember I was very sad for many days when I discovered that in the world there were poor people and rich people; and the strange thing is that the existence of the poor did not cause me as much pain as the knowledge that at the same time there were people who were rich . . . From each year I kept the memory of some injustice that roused me to rebellion.'

But life improved a little when she was ten years old — her mother had finally found another protector. It had taken a while. But despite five children and a growing plumpness, she could still attract men. There was a sexuality, a ripeness about her, an alluring excitement in her flashing, dark eyes. In her late thirties, mature and voluptuous, she had not lacked admirers. But it was finding the right one, the man who could pay *la cuenta* (the bill), that had taken the time. Finally, he appeared in the form of a local, small-town Radical politician. He had met her on a visit to Los Toldos and had promptly fallen for her charms. Like his predecessor, Juan Duarte, he was getting along

14

in years and already had a family. Juana didn't mind that. It showed a stability, lacking in the handsome, young *machos* who had been prowling around her and her daughters in Los Toldos. So he set her up in a small house on Julio A. Roca Street in Junin on the other side of town from his own home. It was not much of a place, built of whitewashed mud brick around a patio, its front door leading directly onto the pavement, typical of an Argentine provincial town. For although Junin boasted a population of over 30,000, it was still very much a town of the pampas — surrounded by the endless plain, the field of corn and herds of cattle.

To Dona Juana's children, moving to Junin from their tiny pueblo was like moving to the big city. There were paved streets, two storey buildings, shops that sold dresses made in Buenos Aires, and even a cinema. Going to the cinema or walking down to the railway station to watch the arrival of the Buenos Aires train provided the main out-of-school entertainment, although in the spring and summer, on warm evenings and lazy Sunday afternoons, the girls would often head for the plaza, where they strolled arm-in-arm in the shade of the broad, leafy ombu trees, giggling and listening to the young men, who circled the other way around the plaza, passing the girls with a *piropo*, a whispered compliment in words that had not changed in generations. To the girl in a green dress: 'You are a miracle when green; what will you be when you are ripe.' Or to the girl in red: 'Pretty as a rose — but I'm afraid of thorns.'

It is doubtful that Eva Duarte had many piropos whispered in her ear. She was still very much of an ugly duckling in those early teenage years. There is an old school picture of her that has survived — a classroom group photograph taken at the end of the school year with the girls in freshly-starched white smocks with bows like butterflies on top of their heads. Eva is half-way back, a rather plain, sullen-looking child with dark, brooding eyes staring unhappily out from a sallow complexion. There's no indication there of the beauty-to-be. Not even a hint of the curves that Argentine girls develop so delightfully at an early age. One of her classmates from those days remembers her as a girl who kept very much to herself, a quiet, day-dreaming type. She was not a bright student, and all the indications were that she faced a depressing future. Her mother had already found husbands for her three eldest girls from the succession of young bachelors who lodged at the house. Elisa married an army officer after finishing high school and getting a job in the post office, thanks to a little string-pulling by Dona Juana's benefactor. Blanca had married a struggling young lawyer, and Arminda married the lift operator at the town hall. Son Juan had picked up a job selling soap on commission to the local stores. As for Eva, mama's plans for her went no further than finishing primary school, then helping out full-time in the boarding house. But her youngest daughter had other ideas. In October of 1933, she had been given a small part in a school play called *Arriba Estudiantes* (Students Arise), an emotional, patriotic, flag-waving melodrama. From that moment on, Eva Duarte resolved to shake the pampas dust from her shoes. She was going to become a great actress.

She did not waste time. The first thing she learned from the film magazines she bought from the *kiosco* at the corner of the plaza was that there was only one place in Argentina where a girl could become a star — Buenos Aires, the nation's capital. That presented certain problems. For a start, there were several hundred miles of pampas between her and the big city. She had no money, and there was certainly no way her family was going to help her. Then, she was still at school, and she was only fourteen years old. But when Eva set her mind on something it was very rare she failed to get it. A few months later, just after her fifteenth birthday, a handsome young tango singer, Agustin Magaldi, came to Junin to play a couple of nights at the local theatre. Juan Duarte had a friend who worked there and who arranged for Eva to slip in through a side door of the theatre during the first night's performance. When Magaldi left the stage, he found this slip of a girl with very white skin and very red lips waiting for him in his makeshift dressing room at the back of the building. The next evening, after the show, they drove through the night to Buenos Aires.

2

AN ASPIRING ACTRESS

For an aspiring young actress, no other city in Latin America offered such a kaleidoscope of opportunity. Buenos Aires in the 1930s was *the* cultural mecca, the leader of the continent's artistic and literary world. There were twenty-five theatres, nine radio stations, and three film companies, all squeezed into the city's compact downtown area of wide avenues and narrow side streets. To the *porteños*, the people who live in the great port on the River Plate, their capital was the Paris of Latin America, a city of beautiful parks, elegant shops, restaurants which were packed until the early hours of the morning, flower sellers, book shops, and pavement cafés; the whole overlaid with an Italianate air, derived from the ornate marble and granite façades of the buildings and the noisy vibrance of the street life.

Eva moved into the heart of theatreland on her very first day in town — taking a room in a cheap hotel just off Calle Corrientes, a street that slashes from west to east across the heart of the city centre. It is the Broadway of Buenos Aires known to porteños as 'the street that never sleeps'. During the day, crowds flock to the banks and stores that line its pavements. At night, while the bankers and shopkeepers sleep, Corrientes changes its image and becomes a neon-lit street of dreams — theatres, cinemas, cabarets, and dance halls —

glittering with excitement and romance until the dawn tarnishes the gilt.

For Eva, the glamour of Calle Corrientes faded quickly, blotted out by the desperate need for a job. She made the rounds of the theatrical agencies. But she had no background, no experience, no references. She dressed badly, and her rough country accent more often than not provoked a smile and a shake of the head among the agents who deigned to see her. She fell nearly three months behind in her rent, and she was reduced to a diet of sandwiches and coffee. Sometimes, she did not even have the few centavos necessary for that.

Her brother Juan, himself now working in a bank in Buenos Aires, tried to persuade her to return to Junin. 'Leave me alone,' she said. 'I know what I'm doing.' She had no intention of leaving. Her will to survive was unbreakable. She told everyone she met that she was going to be Argentina's leading actress — an ambition that must have seemed as ridiculous to the theatrical agents she pestered constantly as if she had announced that one day she was going to be Argentina's First Lady. For she lacked talent, beauty, and charm.

In those humid early summer days of 1935, Eva Duarte's sole preoccupation was getting a job, any job. Indeed, there may well have been moments when she came perilously close to following in the footsteps of so many young peasant girls who arrived in Buenos Aires full of dreams and ambitions, only to finish up in the sleazy brothels down by the waterfront. But in March, just when things were at their darkest, Eva got her first break, a small part in *La Senora de Perez*, a comedy at the Comedia Theatre, starring Eva Franco, one of Argentina's most popular actresses, and Pascual Pelliciota, an actor who quickly replaced her Junin saviour, Magaldi, the tango singer, in her affections. It was the first of a long series of lowly-paid bit parts and short-lived love affairs. The acting jobs never lasted long, either, as it was rare for a play to run for more than a few weeks in Buenos Aires.

In July, she picked up a job in *There's a World in Every Home*. But she was dropped from the company when the play went on tour in the provinces. Then there was a drought until December when she got the part of a laundrywoman in *Madame Sans Gene* for which she received three pesos per night (in those days about 37p). The other members of the cast teased her at rehearsals, testing her dramatic progress by asking her to walk with a book on her head and a lighted candle in her hand. One of the actors in the play remembered her as 'childish, naive, and very romantic', an interesting recollection of a girl whose life was a constant struggle for survival.

In June, 1936, Eva went off on her first provincial tour in a play called *The Mortal Kiss*, about the evils of sexual promiscuity. It was financed by the Argentine Prophylactic League, an organisation of well-meaning, wealthy ladies who believed that they could cut down the illegitimacy rate in Argentina's rural towns with good rousing melodrama. If that was a theme that cut too close to home, the illegitimate girl from Los Toldos needed the money too much to complain about it. Half-way through the trip, however, one of the cast fell ill with an undiagnosed infection. She was sent to hospital and no visitors were allowed. But Eva was determined to show everybody how much she cared for her colleague. She slipped into the hospital and visited her. Inevitably, she became infected, too, and lost her job.

Ill health dogged Eva throughout her life. But she never gave up. That was one thing about which her admirers and enemies could agree. She was quickly back on her feet and making the daily rounds of the theatrical agencies, driving them and her acquaintances mad, begging for parts, any parts, trying anything to charm the influential in the world of the theatre. One of her young contemporaries, Pierina Dealessi, remembers the day when her theatre manager told her there was a girl outside looking for a job. 'We were casting a new play. So I had a chat with her. Evita was a plain girl, very thin, black hair. I asked her if she'd ever worked on the stage before. She told me that she was just back from a provincial tour with Pepita Munoz. We took her on at a miserable salary — 180 pesos a month (about twenty pounds). There were no rest days; besides which we gave four shows on Sunday. We always took a tea break in the middle of the afternoon. Evita drank maté (a relaxing Paraguayan tea drunk out of a gourd through a metal tube). She looked so thin and delicate that I used to add a little milk to her maté to give her some nourishment. She weighed nothing at all. What with hunger, poverty, want, and general neglect, her hands were always cold and damp. We were doing a play called *The Horn of Plenty* by Ricardo Hickens. Evita's part was that of a young, well-dressed lady. She had a beautiful bust but it hung badly because she was so skinny. She once borrowed my stockings to build it up a bit — poor kid. Time and time again I told her — "eat more; don't stay up late, you're in no state to take late nights!" She told me that she had to moonlight other jobs in order to send her mother 700 pesos per month. That was a lot of money in those days. Poor Evita.'

Just how she earned that extra money is one of the many mysteries surrounding Eva Duarte's actress years. Later, she never referred to that period of her life except, vaguely as her 'career as an artiste'. A rumour, never substantiated but long lingering, was that she spent those late evenings in the city's gaudy, noisy nightspots, places like the Tabaris, the Gong, the Embassy, where rich businessmen spent as much on champagne in an evening as a third-rate actress could count herself lucky to earn on the stage in a year. The girls made a tiny percentage on the drinks bought by the men they met at the bar. At closing time, after the final cabaret, Argentine dignity, respectability, and the law, made it impossible for couples to leave the club together. So assignations would be made to meet at nearby amoblado love hotels or the man's garçonnière bachelor apartment. At dawn, the girl would take a taxi home, richer by fifty pesos or so.

Whether Eva went that route or not, she certainly collected a succession of lovers, each one carefully picked to help her career. One of her earliest, most 'helpful' romances began when she was making the rounds during her daily job hunting. It was early in 1937 and she was just eighteen. She called in on *Sintonia Magazine*, which covered theatre and films in typical movie fan magazine style with lots of pictures and breathless reports about the stars and starlets of Argentina's stage and screen. Eva told a friend later that she fell head-over-heels in love with *Sintonia's* owner, a tough former motor racing driver named Emilio Kartulovic, at that very first meeting. It was a romance that did not hurt her. Immediately doors started opening. She got her first job in films, a small part in a fight film called *Seconds out of the Ring*. Gossip had it that during the filming she indulged in a quiet, brief affair with the film's star, Pedro Quartucci.

From then on the threat of hunger disappeared. Jobs were easier to come by, although even she probably realised by then that she was never going to become the great theatrical star of her childhood dreams. She eked out a living with small parts on the stage and in radio. She appeared, briefly, in a few dreadful Argentine films — *The Charge of the Brave* (1939), *The Unhappiest Man in Town* (1940), and *A Sweetheart in Trouble* (1941). And every now and again she landed a modelling assignment for fashion houses and hairdressers. She was learning to take care of her appearance and becoming a good-looking young woman.

She was making enough to move into a better hotel (although she still couldn't afford an apartment) and she even considered having plastic surgery to enlarge her breasts (in crude Argentine macho talk, a girl had to have *melones* (melons) rather than *limones* (lemons) if she wanted to keep a man). But when the day came for the operation, she failed to appear. She had apparently decided to leave nature alone, although the decision may well have been determined by an unexpected setback in her fortunes at about that time. Her brother Juan phoned her to say that he had been caught stealing money at the bank where he worked. It was not a large amount. But if he could not replace it immediately he would go to jail. Eva did not hesitate for a moment. She appeared to have a genuine love for her big brother, despite his playboy ways. She sold everything she had, gave him every peso she possessed and moved back into a cheap boarding house, this time in the Boca, the old Italian district down in the port, where the buildings lean crazily over twisting, narrow alleys leading down to the quayside.

Eva had the steel will of a survivor. Living in the Boca could not have been a pleasant experience for a single girl on her own. In those days in Argentina's big cities, an unchaperoned girl was considered fair game. On the narrow dockside streets, she had to contend with the *chirripos*, the neighbourhood dandies in their tight black suits, gummed-back hair, and highly polished shoes, who lolled their days away in street corner bars, passing leering comments at any girl who passed by. But they quickly learned to respect the backlash of the peasant girl from Los Toldos. 'She had a tongue to skin a donkey,' one of them remembered admiringly years later. Then, after running the gauntlet of the chirripos, Eva would ride the *collectivos*, the fat little buses that rattle round Buenos Aires packed to overflowing (former motor racing world champion Juan Fangio developed his lightning reflexes as a collectivo driver). Eva rarely survived one of those journeys without two or three black pinch marks on her behind. 'Everybody makes a pass at me,' she'd grumble once safely inside the theatre stage door.

The years passed with a gradual improvement in her fortunes. One of the reasons for this was the current prosperity in Buenos Aires. For while war clouds rumbled across Europe and the Pacific in the late 1930s and early 1940s, Argentina was reaping handsome profits from the sale of its beef and grain to countries that had beaten their ploughshares into tanks. In Buenos Aires, the lights burned late and the champagne flowed. The sensual tango moved uptown from the old waterfront bars and flourished in the dance halls along Corrientes. The theatres were packed, and the city's radio stations thrived on the advertising of rich foreign companies — Cinzano, General Electric, Johnson and Johnson, Harrods, Ford, RCA, and many others — whose products impinged on the daily lives of every Argentine. It was during this period, when Eva was in her early twenties, that a wealthy soap manufacturer fell in love with her and gave her a radio programme of her own.

Cesar Marino, head of production at Radio Argentina, recalls that early in 1942, his boss, Roberto Gill, who owned the station, called him into his office and introduced him to Eva Duarte. 'She had obtained the backing of the Radical Soap Company and was looking for a station to put her show on the air. Gill was more interested in the advertiser than the actress, as he'd never met the Duarte girl before, either. "As from now," he told me, "she is going to be our leading star." I didn't know where to begin as the kid was a very, very poor actress. But she was docile, well behaved, nicely-mannered and serious. She always arrived an hour early for rehearsal and left immediately after the broadcast. She never talked to anybody.'

That may have been because Eva was becoming a busy young lady. Besides Radio Argentina, Radio El Mundo was also enjoying her soap-sponsored talents. There, appropriately, she broadcast soap operas with titles like *Love was born when I met you*, and *Love promises*. Later, she also began appearing on Radio Belgrano, where, in January of 1943, she began a radio series that was to make her well-known throughout Argentina. It was called *My Kingdom of Love*, and consisted of weekly soap operas written by a student of philosophy. In them, Eva acted out the lives of famous women in history — Lady Hamilton, Queen Elizabeth I, the Empress Josephine, Madame Chiang Kai-shek, the Tsarina Alexandra of Russia.

The series ran for over a year and was so successful that Eva's picture appeared twice on the cover of *Antena*, a weekly radio newspaper that had one of the largest circulations of any publication in the country. Argentine families bought it primarily for its programme listings. They learned from the coy cover stories about Eva that she loved sentimental waltzes and Greer Garson films. She confessed to being 'a tranquil woman, a homemaker, one who loved family life'. What they did not learn

22

was that the tranquil homemaker had been busily making powerful friends in high places.

In June 1943, a military coup had brought a small group of Army generals to power in Argentina. One evening a month later, Eva picked up the telephone in the dressing room she shared with other actresses at Radio Belgrano. 'Girls,' she said, 'listen to this,' as she dialled a number. 'Hello, is that Government House? Give me President Ramirez.' Then, as the girls gaped, wide-eyed, 'Hello, Mr President. This is Eva Duarte . . . Yes, I'd love to have dinner with you tomorrow evening. At ten. Good. Until then. *Chau*, Pedro.'

Word of the conversation quickly reached the ears of Jaime Yankelevich, the owner of Radio Belgrano. He was a shrewd fat man who had laid the foundation to his fortune in 1923 by cornering the market in the crystal headsets that were needed for the primitive radios of the time. It was just before the world heavyweight boxing championship between Jack Dempsey, the holder of the title, and Argentina's hero, Luis (The Wild Bull of the Pampas) Firpo, and Argentines were rushing to buy radios to listen to the broadcast of the event. So Yankelevich made a fortune. Eva's dinner date prompted him to make another investment. He raised her salary from 150 pesos a month to 5,000. But such uncharacteristic generosity was not prompted by any optimism that a relationship between his young actress and the nation's president would help him. He knew it would not.

President Pedro Ramirez had the reputation of being a hen-pecked husband whose wife kept a very un-Argentine grip on him. On top of that, his stiffness and reactionary ways had earned him the nickname of the 'Little Stick'. So Yankelevich was fairly sure that Eva would not get very far with the president. But he knew something that the other girls in his radio station did not: that Eva already had hooked a member of the military government who was in a position to be much more useful to him. It was Colonel Anibal Imbert, the Minister of Communications, a post which controlled the country's radio stations. The Colonel, a stout little man, had already moved his young, pretty mistress out of the Boca and into a comfortable apartment on Calle Posadas, a quiet, tree-shaded street just off Avenida Alvear, a very fashionable part of Buenos Aires. As far as Jaime Yankelevich was concerned, any girl friend of the man who controlled the life and death of his business was well worth a substantial increase in salary, even if she was a terrible actress.

23

When the other actresses at Radio Belgrano found out about the sudden rise in their colleague's salary, they were more amused than angry. Knowing the reason, they called it Eva's 'official velocity' and they expected her to fall to earth with equal speed as soon as the Colonel dropped her, which the girls, wise to the demi-monde life that most of them lived, knew would be sooner or later. They could not have been more wrong. Eva was on her way to dizzying heights and it was the plump Colonel Imbert who dropped by the wayside, a combination of events that, ironically, he had the misfortune to arrange himself.

On January 15, 1944, an earthquake almost completely destroyed the old Spanish colonial town of San Juan, 500 miles to the west of Buenos Aires. Thousands were killed. In the tremendous wave of sympathy that swept the nation, actors and actresses pounded the streets to collect money to help the survivors. As part of that fund-raising effort, Eva persuaded her lover to stage a monster variety show in Luna Park, a large open-air boxing arena in the centre of Buenos Aires. Leading theatrical and radio stars turned out to perform before a packed audience and a nation-wide hookup of all the country's radio stations.

As the stars mingled on the stage, taking their turns at the microphones, Eva, who had arrived on the arm of Colonel Imbert, caught sight of Libertad Lamarque, one of Argentina's loveliest actresses. She was talking to a tall, handsome army officer. Eva knew who he was — Colonel Juan Domingo Perón. He was rumoured to be the Strongman among the colonels who controlled the military government. She went over to Libertad, whom she knew only slightly, and asked to be introduced. Then, when it was the actress's turn to take the microphone, Eva slipped into the empty chair beside the colonel.

3

AN AMBITIOUS ARMY OFFICER

'I put myself at his side. Perhaps this drew his attention to me and when he had time to listen to me I spoke up as best I could: "If, as you say, the cause of the people is your own cause, however great the sacrifice I will never leave your side until I die."'

That purple passage from *La Razon de mi Vida* is Eva's description of 'the marvellous day' when she met Juan Perón. It sounds more like something out of one of the cheap comic-book romances she liked to read. But what is certainly true is that she wasted no time that first night. It was a warm, spring evening. They slipped away from the rally and drove out of the city to the Tigre, a suburban river resort of muddy delta waterways, tiny islands, boat clubs, mosquitos, and secluded weekend homes hidden away from prying eyes by the purple and orange blossoms of jacaranda trees. The next morning, Eva arrived for work at Radio Belgrano in a War Ministry limousine.

Despite the difference in years — at forty-eight, Perón was exactly double Eva's age — they had a lot in common. For he was a country boy, born on October 8, 1895, on a small pampas farm owned by his father just outside the town of Lobos, 65 miles south of Buenos Aires. Like so many Argentines, his heritage came out of the mass of southern European peasantry that poured into Argentina in the middle 1800s. He claimed that his family name was originally Peroni and that his great-grandfather had been a Sicilian senator. His mother was what is known in Argentina as a *chinita* — a little country girl with Indian blood in her veins, reflected in her son's high cheek bones, ruddy complexion and black eyes.

When he was five years old, the family moved to Patagonia in the deep south of the country. It is a desolate, cold and wind-battered land, hospitable only to sheep. Juan Perón grew up strong and tough, living the life of a gaucho, breaking wild horses, lassoing ostriches with the bolas, fording icy streams in sub-zero weather, riding the stony *mesa*, spurs strapped to his bare feet, his poncho streaming out in the wind. When his father died, his mother kept the ranch and, when he was sixteen packed him off to military college in Buenos Aires where he was an indifferent student but a tough soldier and a brilliant sportsman (he was one of the army's best shots, its fencing champion for sixteen years, and a bare-knuckle fighter much feared in the dockside bars of Buenos Aires during his college years — a bony knob on his right hand tipped off former world heavyweight champion Gene Tunney that he was shaking hands with a man who had used his fists).

He was a handsome, athletic-looking man, over six-foot tall with thick jet-black hair combed back from his forehead, black-brown eyes of shimmering intensity, and a complexion made startlingly florid by a vivid labyrinth of veins on both cheeks. But it was not just his commanding physical appearance that made him the centre of attention in any company. He spoke German, Italian, and a little English, and he was well read, astonishingly so for one who had made the army his whole life. He had personality and charm — a ready smile and a quick wit that drew people to him long before he wielded the sort of power that automatically commanded respectful attention. 'You sat down with Perón and in a few minutes he had won you into his world,' recalled one of his old army friends. 'He'd talk to a young captain, put his arm around his shoulders, and tell him what he wanted to hear. He could convince a socialist that he, too, was a socialist. But then a fascist would talk to him and leave absolutely certain that Perón was a fascist.'

Perón's persuasive powers had worked like magic in the rural isolation of the Andean mountain garrison where had been posted in the summer of 1940. It had not taken him many months to cajole his fellow colonels into joining him in forming a political organisation that would channel their aspirations. Called the GOU, which stood for either Grupo de Oficiales Unidos (United Officers' Group) or its slogan, Gobierno!/ Orden!/Unidad! (Government! Order! Unity!), the officers professed disgust with the corruption of the country's conservative government and resolved to push for a greater say in the affairs of the nation. As secretary of the secret lodge, Perón travelled the country from garrison to garrison, preaching its message to young army officers to whom the talk of national destiny was like red meat and wine.

By the winter of 1943, as thousands of brown-shirted fascists marched almost daily through the streets of Buenos Aires, shouting 'death to the Jews', and 'death to the British pigs', Perón had signed up all but a few hundred of Argentina's 3,600 army officers. He was ready to make his move. On June 4, the government of President Ramon S. Castillo fell like a putrid fruit to a military coup organised by the GOU. The only resistance the army encountered as it rolled into the city with its tanks and armoured trucks was at the Naval School on the outskirts of Buenos Aires, where nearly 100 naval officers and cadets were killed in a futile effort at defence. There was another very brief setback for the GOU when the wrong man, General Arturo Rawson, who had commanded the troops, had, in a moment of exuberance, proclaimed himself president from the balcony of the Casa Rosada, the 'Pink House', the presidential palace in the centre of Buenos Aires. But in a hurried opera-bouffe performance of musical chairs, General Rawson was quickly hustled out the back door of the presidential palace, his place on the balcony taken by the GOU's choice of president, General Pedro P. Ramirez, who had been Minister of War in the Castillo Government.

As General Ramirez donned the presidential sash of office, he admitted in a moment of honest candour that 'among the troops, I have been designated the first soldier'. It was the colonels, of course, who were doing the designating. They appointed one of their own, Colonel Edelmiro Farrell, as Minister of War, the most powerful post in the Cabinet. Colonel Perón, still an unknown figure in the country, took on the post of Under-Secretary at the War Ministry. But, as the Secretary of the GOU, he was the power behind the throne.

President Ramirez was a weak 'Little Stick' and he found himself buffeted back and forth between the various factions jockeying for power in the army. He became a bit of a joke to the porteños of Buenos Aires who quickly realised that their president was the pawn of others.

One of the stories going the rounds at the time poked fun at the executive decrees that poured out of the Casa Rosada in an endless stream. Apparently, a man had been sitting in his bathroom idly tearing off yards of toilet paper which he floated out of the window and across the nearby Plaza de Mayo. A detachment of soldiers came banging on his door, their officer demanding to know if the man had been responsible for the paper barrage. He admitted it. 'Then it's the concentration camp for you,' he was told. 'But why,' asked the astonished porteño as he was led away. 'Because all that paper floated in the window of the Casa Rosada and the President has been signing it.'

Ramirez knew about the jokes. He was no fool, and he tried to resign. But he was roughly told by Perón that 'you can't resign until we are ready to let you go.' His political impotence was already being noted by foreign news correspondents based in Buenos Aires. On October 31, just four months after the revolution, John W. White of the *New York Herald Tribune* cabled from Santiago, Chile (he couldn't file from Buenos Aires because of press censorship), that 'the guiding mind behind the Ramirez regime is an intelligent and ruthless but almost unknown young colonel named Juan Perón.'

By then, President Ramirez was already well aware that he had to break Perón or remain his puppet. But he had been powerless to prevent the colonel from setting himself up with an additional power base as head of a brand new ministry, the Secretariat of Labour and Welfare. It was not a Cabinet post because the Argentine Constitution limited the number of ministries to eight and the quota was already filled. But Perón made it clear straight away that he had big plans for the Secretariat. The duties of the new department, he announced, would be to 'strengthen national unity by securing greater social justice and an improvement in the standard of living of Argentine.' Many years later, he looked back upon 'the day we created the Secretariat of Labour and Welfare was for me the first day of our movement. From that mement the revolution acquired a new meaning and began to travel down a road from which there was no turning back.'

The first step along that road took him into the headquarters of the country's unions. Their leaders quickly found out that they went to jail if they failed to show proper enthusiasm for Perón. To make sure they all got the message an example was made of Jose Tesorieri, the secretary of the Union of Government Employees. He was gaoled because he signed a petition asking the government to break diplomatic relations with Germany, an attitude that was, of course, anathema to Perón. After five months of brutal softening up in the Villa Devoto gaol in Buenos Aires, Tesorieri was released and restored to his job on the condition, which he accepted, that he speak for Perón at public meetings. He really had no choice. His wife and children had been forced to live on charity while he was inside. Not surprisingly, union leaders throughout the country were soon organising 'spontaneous' demonstrations on Perón's behalf. 'He has thrown himself into his work with such a will,' reported *New York Times* correspondent Arnold Cortesi, 'that he has aroused not a little jealousy among his colleagues who suspect him of promoting his own popularity.'

President Ramirez did not just suspect. He was convinced of it. On January 26, 1944, with the support of senior Navy officers who despised Perón, believing him responsible for the slaughter of the young naval cadets at the start of the revolution, the President signed a decree breaking diplomatic relations with Germany, knowing full well that would cause a make-or-break crisis with Perón. But nothing happened for a couple of weeks. The reason for that may have been because the colonel had just met the delightful Eva Duarte and, possibly, he was finding it hard to keep his mind on affairs of state. But then he also knew just where the power lay and it was not over in the Casa Rosada where the president sat. Calling a group of friendly reporters into his office at the Labour Secretariat, he told them: 'This is the government of the GOU, and I am the GOU. In my desk I have the signed, undated resignations of 3,300 of the army's 5,600 officers, and the others do not matter.'

Still rumours of coups and counter-coups were sweeping the Argentine capital almost daily. Then, on February 15, the president made his next move. He leaked word that he was about to declare war on Germany. That stirred Perón into action. All morning, groups of officers moved in and out of the Labour Secretariat to discuss the crisis with their undisputed leader. A decision reached, a dozen of the younger army officers, lieutenants and captains, walked over to the Foreign Ministry, drew their swords and chased the Foreign Minister and his Under-Secretary out of the building. At that point, President Ramirez promptly abandoned his plan to declare war on Germany, and for the next few days nothing happened while portenos, used to this kind of thing by now, went about their daily business, exchanging rumour for rumour. Finally, on February 24, Ramirez played his last card. He sent a messenger over to Perón's office with a demand for his resignation. The burly colonel fixed the messenger with a steely gaze and told him: 'inform the wretches who sent you that they will never get me out of here alive.'

That night, armed soldiers seized the central telephone exchange in Buenos Aires. All communications with foreign countries were immediately cut. Another contingent occupied the central post office. An entire mechanised infantry regiment descended upon police headquarters and disarmed the police force, which only a few hours earlier had been armed with rifles and ammunition. More truckloads of troops rolled through the suburbs to the presidential residence in Olivos, where sentries with fixed bayonets were posted around the building. In the early hours of the morning, Juan Perón and five other colonels arrived at the residence, burst into the president's study and forced him at gunpoint to resign. Then Perón returned to the city and the heavily-guarded War Ministry, where he and his friend, Vice-President Farrell, had set up their operations' headquarters. It was three o'clock in the morning. But there were still reporters around, taking in the excitement and confusion and trying to find out what was going on. Perón feigned surprise at seeing them. 'No pasa nada,' (nothing's happening), he told them jovially. But then a touch of concern crept into his voice. 'The poor president is tired, very tired.' A few hours later, an official communique announced that President Ramirez, being too fatigued to continue the arduous duties of the presidency, had delegated his duties to Vice-President Farrell.

The new president was no more his own boss than Ramirez had been. In fact, it was so obvious that he was Perón's front man that he became the target of even more irreverent jokes than his predecessor among the porteno population of Buenos Aires. In one story, the hapless president dropped his handkerchief while reviewing a march-past of troops. Picking it up, he whispered to another general. 'You don't know how much that handkerchief means to me, it's the only thing Perón will let me get my nose into. Nicknamed 'the Phantom' because Hollywood's *The Phantom of the Opera* opened in Buenos Aires the day of his inauguration, he slipped quickly into the background as Perón moved aggressively to the front of Argentina's political stage.

Most of the unkind stories usually reached the President's ears. 'It's said that Colonel Perón and I quarrel every day,' he grumbled to a friend, 'and that I don't dare leave my office because someone might be sitting in my chair when I get back. But it's all lies.' And so it probably was. For Perón was quite content to let the president make a public fool of himself while he continued to build his own power base. In a memorable speech that was echoed nearly three decades later in Vietnam by an American army officer who said, straight-faced, 'We had to destroy the village to save it,' President Farrell told the Argentine people: 'We must be tyrants to make the people freer.'

Freedom for the people was certainly the last thing on Perón's mind at that time. In July 1944, when seventeen generals signed a memorandum demanding that the government restore civilian constitutional government through elections, lift the state of siege which the country had been under since the revolution, and order all military officers to relinquish government positions and return to their barracks, Perón immediately promoted seventeen colonels to the rank of general, thus giving himself absolute control of Argentina's military establishment. Soon afterwards, he had President Farrell promote him to Vice-President, a post he held with that of War Minister and Secretary of Labour. To cheering crowds of workers assembled in the Plaza de Mayo, Perón declared from the balcony of the Casa Rosada that, 'I display only three titles: that of being a soldier, that of being considered the first Argentine worker, and that of being a patriot.' Down below in the Plaza, the humblest, poorest of the population, hatless, coatless, tieless, their dark skins and high cheekbones betraying their Indian blood, roared out 'Perón, Perón,' a battle-cry that was to reverberate across the nation for years to come.

They had not taken up the cry of 'Evita' yet. Eva Duarte's relationship with the Vice-President had not surfaced publicly. People in government and high society knew about it, of course. But it was not a matter of much concern. 'Having a love affair might ruin an American politician,' remarked a former US ambassador to the Argentine, James Bruce, who was stationed there at the time. 'But not having one might make a Latin politician suspect. The names of favoured mistresses of important Argentines are generally open secrets and no one regards it as at all unusual.' However, there were a few raised eyebrows when a story circulated that Eva had marched round to Perón's apartment only a few days after she had met him and had thrown out his teenage mistress, a girl from the northern provinces whom Perón had lovingly nicknamed Piranha after the fierce, tiny fish with razor-like teeth that inhabit some of Argentina's inland rivers. The piranha proved to be no match for the older woman.

Knowing her lover's reputation as a man with a roving eye, Eva promptly moved him into an apartment next door to hers in the same building in Calle Posados in order to keep a closer watch on him. Every morning, an army conscript turned up with a can of fresh milk from the nearest army barracks, and it was usually Perón, in his dressing gown, who opened the door to take it in. That raised a few more eyebrows, particularly among the wives of senior army officers. For in polite Argentine society, a man did not live with his mistress. They persuaded their husbands to complain to Perón about the notoriety, the lack of dignity, of the Vice-President of the nation living openly with an actress. He laughed at them. He was, he told them, a man of normal appetites, adding with sardonic humour, 'How much better than if, as with some officers I know, it was said that I was being seen with actors.'

If there was a suggestion that the relationship could hurt Perón's career, it could do nothing but good for Eva's. Although her influential friends had done nothing to improve her acting — 'She was terrible, cold as an iceberg, incapable of stirring an audience,' recalled one of her old acting colleagues, Pierina Dealessi — it had done wonders for her earning power. Jaime Yankelevitch at Radio Belgrano had raised her salary again, estimating that Eva's switch from her old lover, Colonel Imbert, to a new one, Colonel Perón, was well worth a few thousand extra pesos a month. So between Radios Belgrano, El Mundo, and El Estado, Eva by mid-1944 was earning the equivalent of £1,800 a month, a fortune by Argentine standards.

Pierina, who used to work with her at Radio Belgrano, said that Yankelevitch was very demanding of his star performer, trying to squeeze out the very last drop of her not very considerable talent. One day, he went too far, and Eva refused to go back. Terrified that her powerful friends would close him down, Yankelevitch pleaded with Pierina: 'Ask your god for help. I can't get any help from mine.' But peace was finally restored, and Eva returned. Her colleagues were extremely envious of her intimacy with Perón. Pierina remembered Malisa Zini, a popular radio actress of the time, saying to her: 'I just saw Perón on the street. If only Evita would lend him to me — just for fifteen minutes.'

But Eva had other plans for Perón. All her experience told her that her position as mistress of the most powerful man in the country was a precarious one because it was rare in Argentina that a man married his mistress. At the same time, she also knew herself well enough to realise that her interest in him would last only as long as he remained the powerful figure that he was, and the chances on that score were not too good, either: there had been three presidents and forty ministers in the past eighteen months. So, very simply, she decided to keep his love by seeing to it that he stayed in power.

Shortly after Perón moved into Apartment 'B' in Calle Posadas, Apartment 'A' replaced the presidential palace as the centre of power in Argentina. His kitchen cabinet — army cronies and men he had appointed to key positions in the trade unions — met there daily, and Eva's involvement in these sessions went a great deal further than brewing the maté and pouring the whisky.

As a girl from the pueblo, she knew there was a source of power in the land that had not been tapped since the days of 'bloody' Rosas. He had been the first gaucho among gauchos. But now the men of the plains had poured into the cities. Nearly a third of Argentina's population of approximately 14 million lived in and around Buenos Aires by the early 1940s, and well over sixty per cent of those people were poor, many of them living in the *villa miserias*, the squalid shanty 'towns of misery' that had sprung up on the outskirts of the capital. For years, electoral fraud had deprived them of any say in the running of the country. What Perón had to do, Eva insisted, was to become their leader, to become, in the style of Rosas, the first worker among workers.

The two of them criss-crossed the country, holding mass meetings in the great granary centres of Rosario and Santa Fé, in the new industrial city of Cordoba, the vinyards of Mendoza, and out into the remote rural regions, provinces like Salta and Corrientes, where dark-skinned mestizo peasants lived a life of poverty that had hardly changed in a hundred years. In Buenos Aires, they spent evenings visiting working class neigh-bourhood *barrios* — the old docklands of La Boca, which Eva knew so well, and the slaughterhouse district of Avellaneda as well as some of the roughest and grimmest of the villa miserias. After back-thumping *abrazos* with new-found friends

33

in the *boliches*, the neighbourhood bar/restaurants, they drank *vino común*, cheap, throat-rasping red wine, and talked and argued politics until the early hours of the morning. Industrial workers, many of them toiling fourteen-hour days in desperation to feed and clothe their families, suddenly found, for the first time in their lives, powerful people who would not only listen to them but would actually do something.

From his Ministry of Labour, Perón decreed minimum wages and decent living conditions for the country's agricultural workers, raising them, at the stroke of a pen, from their feudal peonage. This, naturally, provoked howls of outrage from the wealthy estancieros, who had to pay the increases from their pockets. But Perón was unmoved. He later wrote: 'The unrestricted ambitions of the conservative classes to keep everything for themselves blinded them to the evidence: whoever wishes to keep everything will lose everything.' More decrees streamed from his office. White collar workers, shop assistants, and factory hands obtained wage increases, some of 50 per cent or more. He gave them four-week holidays, sick leave, protection from arbitrary dismissal, all unheard of before in Argentina. And he invented the most popular of all perks, the *aguinaldo*, the thirteenth month wage handed to every worker just before Christmas.

Employers grumbled bitterly. But, as Perón well knew, they were not about to go bankrupt. Leaving aside the fact that they had exploited their workers for far too long, both they and the nation as a whole were enjoying a wave of unprecedented prosperity. The country's export trade was booming with post-war Europe willing to pay any price for Argentina's beef and wheat. As larger and larger credit balances piled up month after month, the peso became one of the world's strongest currencies, a prosperity reflected in the boom-town atmosphere of Buenos Aires with its crowded stores, restaurants, theatres and nightclubs. In the summer resort town of Mar del Plata, the world's largest casino (with fifty-six roulette tables) kept its wheels spinning day and night to mop up the money of wealthy free-spending Argentines.

But for the first time this wealth was also beginning to seep down to ordinary working people, thanks to Perón. Understandably, bus drivers, lorry drivers, wine workers, sugar workers, metal workers, road workers flocked into the unions Perón formed under one giant umbrella organisation, the Confederacion General del Trabajo (CGT — the General

Confederation of Labour). Trade union leaders who failed to fall into line were unceremoniously packed off to concentration camps in Patagonia. At least 130 socialist and communist union bosses were jailed, and union members who demonstrated and struck in protest were threatened in no uncertain terms by Perón that they would join their leaders if they did not mend their ways. They soon did. By mid-1945, Perón could safely boast that he had an army of four million workers at his back.

Even the obstreperous meat packing house workers fell in love with Perón. Their case was one of the grimmest among the oppressed poor of Argentina. They had struggled for decades to improve their pittance wages and abominable working conditions in the stench of the slaughter yards. They had hoped that the nationalistic military regime would help them in the battle with their British and American employers. But not even the military was willing to interfere with an industry so vital to the nation's economy. It was the country's biggest industrial employer by far. Yet its 60,000 workers possessed neither economic or political strength.

The top union leader of the meat packers Jose Peter, a brilliant and forceful communist, angrily exposed packing house companies that ignored the few labour laws that existed and laid off workers without reason. Union organisers were black-listed and beaten up. But what incensed the workers most was the method by which the companies paid them. Called the 'standard' system, workers had to perform a set amount of labour or be fired. After they had reached that daily standard, they were then paid on a declining scale. When productivity rose, as it did because of the workers' desperate efforts to earn enough to keep their families alive, the companies simply raised the minimum level for payment. It was a classic treadmill — no matter how fast they went, it did them no good in the end.

Perhaps more than anything else the 'standard' explains why the Peróns captured the imagination, support and fervent loyalty of the working people of Argentina. In many ways it typified an essential element of Argentine society — the casual, brutal lack of sensitivity by employer towards employee. As Jose Peter described the horror of it: 'It converts the workers into much less than a machine; because a machine is given rest, it is oiled, it is cared for and repaired, while only illness and un-employment are left to the worker after the standard . . . has extracted his last drop of energy and ruined his health. The standard system has managed to make the worker lose even the faculty for thought. Not to be able to read, except with a great deal of effort. To lose interest in life. Not even to want to go to the movies, or take a walk. To await the horrible hour of work in agony. To beg for the hour of payment. To lose the possibility of sleep, because the barbaric rhythm of the standard takes over the nerves . . . The labourer is turned into a shadow of his former self. Tuberculosis, rheumatism, insomnia, mental ruin, a permanent picture of misery and helplessness, a tenement house, hungry children, a consumptive wife. This is what the standard signifies.'

So the meat packing workers struck, and human blood flowed through the gutters of the slaughter-house district south of the Riachuelo River as police and employers combined to crush the strike. Then something happened that the workers could hardly believe. In the midst of the fighting and sniping, Colonel Juan Perón, the country's Vice-President, walked through the streets of Avellaneda arm-in-arm with his pretty girl friend, Eva Duarte, whom they had all heard on the radio, and their own Cipriano Reyes, a burly, young union organiser. Word spread through the district: 'Perón is with us.' The next day, he brought the strike to a compulsory end, ordering the packing houses to re-employ every worker they had fired and to increase wages by 30 per cent with a guaranteed 60 hours of work every two weeks, thus putting an end to the hated 'standard' system. The workers showed their gratitude by deserting their old communist leader, Jose Peter, for Perón's friend, Cipriano Reyes, and his new union, the Federation of Labour Unions of the Meat Industry, which for the first time brought all the industry's workers together into one pro-Perón organisation.

4

EVA TO THE RESCUE

The early months of 1945 were not good ones for Perón and Eva. They finally realised they had picked a loser in Nazi Germany, and their humiliation was rubbed in by Winston Churchill who commented: 'They have chosen to dally with evil but not only with evil but with the losing side.' Their country stood friendless in the world. And, understandably, relations with the Americans were the worst they had ever been; President Franklin D. Roosevelt pointedly remarked on 'the extraordinary paradox of the growth of Nazi-Fascist influence and the increasing application of Nazi-Fascist methods in a country of this hemisphere at the very time that these forces of aggression and oppression are drawing ever closer to the hour of defeat.' In undiplomatic language, the US Ambassador to Argentina, Spruille Braden, referred to the military regime as one 'which in common honesty no one could call anything but fascist, and typically fascist.' Angrily, Perón responded: 'Some say that what I am doing follows the policy of Nazism. All I can say is this: If the Nazis did this, they had the right idea.' When his hero, Benito Mussolini was executed by Italian partisans, he defiantly eulogised him: 'Mussolini was the greatest man of this century, but he committed certain disastrous errors. I, who have the advantage of his precedent before me, shall follow in his footsteps but also avoid his mistakes.' To make sure the

Argentines did not get ideas about one precedent, Perón banned all newsreel film that showed Mussolini's body hanging by the heels alongside that of his mistress.

The sympathy of the country's middle-classes, numbering at least five million in Buenos Aires alone — had been overwhelmingly on the side of the Allies, no doubt because of the country's historic ties with Britain and France, which proved far too strong to be broken by their government's pro-Nazi propaganda. In fact, the end of the war triggered such a powerful tide of sentiment for democracy in the press, in the universities, and on the street that it threatened to swamp Perón.

On the day Japan surrendered, bringing World War II to an end, thousands of Argentines marched cheering through the centre of the city, only to be waylaid by several hundred armed soldiers, shouting their own slogans, 'Long live Perón!' 'Death to democracy!' and 'Down with the Jews!' Two students died in the clashes, which Perón promptly blamed on the country's tiny Communist Party.

However, public resistance seemed to grow. Thousands of young students — in Buenos Aires, Cordoba, La Plata, and Tucuman — barricaded themselves in their universities and held off tear gas attacks by riot police for over a week. As each campus fell, youngsters fought from room to room, using desks and chairs as weapons. In Buenos Aires, the boys were dragged off to interrogation centres and the girls to San Miguel Prison, which was normally only used for holding prostitutes. By the beginning of October, the number of political prisoners topped the four thousand mark and was still rising as busloads of detainees swept daily into Buenos Aires' Villa Devoto Prison, the military gaol on Marin Garcia island in the River Plate, and the bleak Neuquen Prison in the Andean foothills. When the gaols bulged so they could take not more, the police requisitioned private houses, packing prisoners into tightly shuttered mansions in the suburbs.

The threat of civil war still hung in the air. Eva Duarte took to carrying a grenade in her handbag, while her lover defiantly proclaimed: 'Everybody is demanding my head, but thus far no one has come to get it.'

He spoke too soon. Some of his fellow officers had finally had enough. But, ironically, it was not Perón's heavy-handed dictatorship which provoked them into plotting his downfall. They simply could not stand his girl friend. They had watched with mounting embarrassment and anger as Perón turned more and more to Eva Duarte for political advice. As soldiers, they were supposed to be running a military dictatorship. Yet a woman pulled the strings. It outraged their sense of dignity and their masculine pride. No Argentine dared laugh at them, of course, at least not to their faces, anyway. But they were uncomfortably aware that ribald cartoons undermining their authority had appeared in the newspapers of neighbouring countries.

The final indignity, as far as they were concerned, came when Eva arranged for her mother's latest boy friend, a postal clerk named Oscar Nicolini, to become Director of Posts and Telegraph, a position once held by her first military lover, Colonel Imbert. No sooner had Nicolini taken over his new job, than Eva moved right in to the office next to his. There was no doubt in the minds of senior army officers that Colonel Perón's mistress had deftly placed herself in control of all of the nation's communications. They were not going to tolerate it. She had to go.

On October 9th, two senior generals arrived at his War Ministry office shortly before mid-day. One of them was an old friend of Perón's, Carlos von der Becke, whom he had appointed Army Chief of Staff, promoting him from Brigadier General to General of Division. But on this morning, Perón had no time for the usual courtesies between friends. Bluntly, he asked him what the decision was. Von der Becke stuttered, shuffled his feet and abruptly turned and walked out of the office, leaving it to his colleague, General Juan Pistarini, the Minister of Works, to break the bad news that someone finally had come to get his head, that his friend whom he had placed in the Casa Rosada had betrayed him and gone over to the enemy.

'The President feels that you should resign,' said Pistarini nervously. Perón did not blink, though the shock must have been considerable. He summoned his ADC. 'Bring me a sheet of paper to write out my resignation.' Then he wrote: 'His Excellency the President of the Nation: I hereby resign my position as Vice-President, Minister of War and Secretary of Labour and Welfare, with all of which Your Excellency has deigned to honour me.' He signed and handed the note to Pistarini. 'I've written it in my own hand,' he said, 'so all can see that my hand has not trembled.'

The news flashed around the world. 'Perón resigns all powers after Argentine army coup' headlined the *New York Times*. In Washington, the State Department refused comment 'pending confirmation'. But in Buenos Aires, thousands of porteños made their comment as they streamed through the central streets of the city, shouting 'We want his head!' Champagne flowed over at Naval Headquarters, where the hatred of Perón went much deeper than anything felt by the army. The senior Navy man, Vice-Admiral Hector Vernengo Lima, Chief of Naval Operations, believed strongly that Perón's downfall provided a timely opportunity for the military to get out of politics. But the Army had its doubts about that.

As the country's top military leaders met in continuous session at the presidential residence in Olivos to sort out their country's future, it quickly became obvious that the generals were terrified of what could happen to them if civilians regained political power. They feared that the army would be exposed to reprisals, or at least to measures aimed at ensuring that military revolutions like that of 1943 would never happen again. General Avalos, the leader of the coup against Perón, considered it imperative that the next president should be an Army man. As he had just appointed himself Minister of War in Perón's place and was clearly the man with the power, his army colleagues felt he should be the next president. They brushed aside Navy suggestions that the government be turned over to the Supreme Court until the election of a civilian president. But while they quarrelled over the spoils of victory, they forgot to keep a watch on the man they had removed from power.

Perón left the War Ministry right on the heels of Generals Von der Becke and Pistarini and hurried home to Eva's apartment on Calle Posadas, finding to his surprise that she was there waiting for him. She already knew what had happened. For news travels fast in Buenos Aires, sometimes faster than the event. In fact, she had found out in a most unpleasant way. Turning up for work at Radio Belgrano, she had been called into the office of a contented-looking Jaime Yankelevich.

'Your boy friend has been sacked,' he told her, brutally drawing a finger across his throat. 'You're out, too,' he added. Eva did not wait to hear any more. She fled. She was still seething when Perón arrived.

'That son of a bitch,' she kept on repeating, 'And after all I've done for him.' But she quickly turned her attention to the real cause of her crisis — her lover's downfall. 'What are you going to do?' she asked. Peron shrugged. There was not much he could do, he told her. He certainly was not going to start a civil war, even if his friends in the army were prepared to do battle for

Above: Juana Ibarguren who gave birth to five illegitimate children, the youngest of whom was Maria Eva.

Below: A pampas rancho, typical of the one-room home in which Evita was born.

Above: First Communion: Evita is on the left. Sister Elisa is next to her; sister Blanca is in the centre at the back, and brother Juancito is on Blanca's left.

Below: Evita, aged 14, a picture taken from her sixth grade class photo.

Above: Her first big picture. Feuding on the set resulted in Libertad Lamarque having to flee into exile when Evita came to power.

Below: A scene from Circus Cavalcade. Everybody who saw Evita act agreed that she was a terrible actress.

Above: The young star posing.

Below: A little light music in the apartment she shared with her next-door neighbour, Col. Perón.

him, and he was not so certain of that any more as some of those friends, like Becke and Farrell, had already deserted him. Perón was ready to give up. But Eva was not prepared to let him.

First, she screamed at him, telling him to pull himself together and act like a man. Then she got to work on the telephone. Within an hour, scores of young captains and colonels, all men promoted by Perón, began streaming in to the apartment, past the heavy guard that had been thrown up around the building by a loyal detachment of officer cadets from the Military College. Eva had calculated that with the army divided in its loyalties and with the chain of military command hopelessly confused at the top, it was the junior officers, the men who actually controlled the troops, who counted. They owed their careers to Perón, she reminded them, and now it was time for them to show their loyalty, not only to Perón but to the ordinary people of Argentina who had finally found someone willing to work to lift them from their poverty and misery. She played on the themes that make a young officer's heart race — heroism, patriotism. The very destiny of the nation was in their hands, she told them. It was a performance of skill, emotion, and warmth — all qualities she had so lacked on the stage — from a beautiful, impassioned woman. Not a single officer left that apartment without first pledging his allegiance in ringing tones.

It went on all evening and through most of the next day, the tiny apartment filling and emptying, with groups of officers arriving bewildered and angry, leaving half an hour later pumped full of Eva Duarte's adrenalin. Early that evening of the 10th, she sent Perón off to the Labour and Welfare Ministry on the pretext of collecting personal papers from his office. While he was there, wandering around the building, bidding emotional farewells to clerks and typists as well as top ministry bureaucrats, Eva was on the phone again — this time to union officials pleading with them to get as many of their members over to the Labour Ministry as quickly as possible. Their beloved leader was there. Now that he had been thrown out of his job because he had done so much for the workers, he would speak to them one last time before going into retirement.

Next, she phoned her mother's lover, Oscar Nicolini, who was sitting fearfully in his office in the Central Post Office, waiting to be fired. Bluntly, she told him that if he wanted to hang on to his job, he had better listen carefully to her instructions and carry them out immediately. Her Juan was at the Labour

41

Ministry. A large crowd of workers was gathering outside. He would probably talk to them when he left the ministry for the last time. The state radio network must carry that talk, she told Nicolini, and broadcast it live throughout Argentina by hooking in to every radio station in the country.

Finally, she called Federal Police Headquarters. Her friend, Colonel Velazco, the Police Chief, had been fired minutes after Perón had resigned. But the whole police department was militantly pro-Perón. Eva was listened to respectfully when she suggested that the Buenos Aires newspapers which had enthusiastically reported Perón's resignation — nearly all of them — should be closed for mentioning troop movements while the nation was under a state of siege.

Throughout that evening, Argentina was given its first demonstration of the nation-wide power of Eva Duarte, though few people realised it at the time. Police squads raided and closed newspapers in every major city in the country. All the evening newspapers in Buenos Aires were shut down. Great crowds began to gather around the Ministry of Labour. When the numbers had reached close to 30,000 packing the side streets as well as the main avenue in front of the building, Perón walked out on to the street, where, not by coincidence, radio microphones had already been set up. Dressed in civilian clothes and bareheaded, he told the vast throng packed in around him that he was a simple citizen now, to which there were roars of 'No, no, no. We want you back!'

However, he had an announcement to make, he said. Before leaving his office, he had signed a decree granting all Argentine workers salary increases and a share of the profits of the companies for which they worked. There were great cheers at that. But then there was a hush as he warned them to be prepared for war. 'If you the workers are decided to defend your conquests, I am going to defend you against the oligarchy of capitalist interests. Follow my leadership and victory will be ours.' There was more cheering, and the crowd set out through the streets, shouting 'Perón for President!' Mounted policemen, who the day before had charged people expressing their joy at Perón's resignation, now chased away any one who attempted to interfere with the marching workers. Even more significantly, Perón's speech had been carried live, as Eva had planned it, on every radio station in Argentina. It hardly sounded like the last farewell of a deposed dictator.

Out at Campo de Mayo, officers listened to the speech in

astonishment and then fury. The gall of the man! He was finished. They had his resignation in their hands. Their military might controlled the country, and yet he was still acting as though he ran things. Three hundred of them marched to the living quarters of General Avalos and demanded to speak to him although he had already retired for the night. They got him out of bed and told him they were marching on Buenos Aires to throw out General Farrell from the Casa Rosada. They were also going to seize Perón and toss him in gaol if they did not string him up from the nearest lamp-post first. They were enraged that he had been allowed to make a speech over the state radio and even more incensed that newspapers had been suspended for reporting military details of the coup, details which had been supplied by them.

General Avalos finally calmed them down with a promise that as soon as he was sworn in as the new War Minister the next morning he would order Perón's arrest. But that was easier said than done. For after his broadcast on the evening of the 11th, Juan, with Eva, had slipped out of town and headed towards the Tigre, the river resort at the mouth of the delta of the River Plate. From there, the two of them took a launch and cruised through the narrow reed-choked waterways to the tiny island and cottage where they had made love the night they first met. The next day, undisturbed, they enjoyed the warm spring sunshine, listening on their radio to the chaos they had left behind in the city.

For a while that morning, Argentina had been reduced to a government of three men, President Farrell, General Avalos, and Admiral Vernengo Lima, who had taken the post of Navy Minister. The rest of the Cabinet had resigned, and President Farrell had offered his resignation, too. But the garrison at Campo de Mayo refused to let him go. For his departure would have left the country without a President or Vice-President and that would have meant, according to the Constitution, the handing over of the government's powers to the Supreme Court, a civilian body. That was the last thing the garrison officers wanted. They were determined to keep the government in military hands, and they were sure they had sufficient fire power outside the gates of the city to see that they got what they wanted.

It was not what President Farrell wanted. Marooned in the presidential residence in Olivos, he was still trying to prevent the arrest of his good friend, Juan Perón. So he was not willing to appoint new ministers until Perón's safety was guaranteed. However, over at the Circulo Militar, the Military Officers' Club, a massive baroque mansion overlooking Plaza San Martin, the country's top generals and admirals had decided that the only sensible political solution lay in President Farrell's resignation and the delivery of his powers to the Supreme Court.

As officers scurried in and out of the club, a large crowd gathered across the street under the shade of the Plaza's acacia trees. It is an elegant part of downtown Buenos Aires, perched on a hillock, once the site of a slave market, looking out towards the River Plate. Two of the city's most fashionable streets, Avenida Santa Fé and Càlle Florida, meet at Plaza San Martin, which exudes an air of established wealth in the grey, old converted *palacios* of the oligarchy, which was what the Circulo Militar once was.

The people in the plaza also fitted in with their surroundings. They were mostly middle-class — businessmen, lawyers, doctors, housewives, respectable clerks from the city's financial district a few blocks away — all well dressed, very different from the workers who had cheered Perón outside the Labour Ministry the night before. But they were just as noisy, singing the songs and shouting the catchwords that had become fashionable during the recent months of opposition to the military government. There was a moment of near panic, however, when the dreaded mounted police appeared on the scene, warning the crowd to disperse or face the consequences. But, dramatically, a young officer in uniform appeared on the club balcony and warned the commander of the police that if he gave the order to charge the crowd, all the officers in the club would themselves lead the people against them. The mounted police promptly wheeled and trotted out of the square into the narrow, hilly side streets. A few minutes later, Admiral Lima appeared on the balcony to tell the crowd, which by now had grown to close on 50,000, that the military had discarded the idea of turning over the government to the Supreme Court. But he promised them that Argentina would soon have a civilian government. There were loud boos and shouts of 'We have heard such promises from Perón.' The Admiral replied with studied dignity: 'I am not Perón. I am Admiral Vernengo Lima.'

But that did not sooth tempers, which were getting more and more frayed in the plaza as it became apparent that the military had no intention of giving up power. Army officers were manhandled and cursed as they struggled through the crowd to the club and they were booed each time they appeared in the window. Someone splashed the words 'For Rent' in red paint across the wall of the club. Another added: 'To the gallows with Perón.' As dusk fell, a trumpet sounded in one of the side streets. Suddenly, the hated police were back, charging into the crowd, swinging sabres and firing blank cartridges. In the panic, men and women fought for shelter, under the marble benches in the plaza, behind the acacia trees, against doorways, and in the sanctuary of the plush foyer of the Plaza Hotel. Then street battles began as civilians started sniping at the police and the police abandoned their horses and sabres for armoured cars, rifles and sub-machine guns. Miraculously, there were only two deaths despite all the shooting that took place, although close to 100 people were injured, some seriously. Once again, the responsibility for the brutality lay with the pro-Perón senior police officers, who took advantage of the absence of their new police chief who had driven to the Tigre on a tip that Perón was hiding in the islands.

The new police chief, accompanied by naval officers, finally found Perón at one o'clock in the morning, asleep in the cottage with Eva. The colonel started to shake when he was told that he was going to be taken to a gunboat on the River Plate. He was terrified. The Navy hated him, he knew that. He had never been forgiven for the slaughter of the young naval cadets during the revolution two years before. He was convinced he was going to be killed, and he begged for mercy. Eva, on the other hand, flew into an uncontrollable rage. She screamed obscenities, shouted insults, and spat in the faces of the three shocked Navy officers. Perón they could handle. They told him they were not going to kill him. But he was still shaking. So they sat him down and gave him a whisky while Eva continued to scream at them. They had been told to arrest her, too. But they did not know what to do. They were accustomed to the etiquette of gentlemen. They had no idea how to handle the hysterical blonde who was threatening to attack them physically if they did not get out. They got out, pushing a stumbling, bemused Perón in front of them, leaving Eva behind. It was an error of judgement that was to change the course of Argentine history.

Eva wasted no more time on tears. She rushed back to Buenos Aires and began phoning the trade union friends that she and Perón has so assiduously cultivated. But the 13th and 14th of October were a Saturday and Sunday, which almost certainly meant that she accomplished little on those two days. Argentines do not make revolutions on weekends or during the summer holiday period — from Christmas to the end of February. They are too busy enjoying themselves. To them, revolutions, like work, are the business of ordinary weekdays. So it was not until Monday the 15th that Eva began to rally support for her counter-revolution. In her autobiography, she claimed that 'I flung myself into the streets searching for those friends who might still be of help to him . . . As I descended from the neighbourhoods of the proud and rich to those of the poor and humble, doors were opened to me more generously and with more warmth. Above I found only cold and calculating hearts, the "prudent" hearts of "ordinary" men incapable of thinking or doing anything extraordinary, hearts whose contact nauseated, shamed and disgusted one.'

She had certainly felt that way about the rich all her life. But it is more likely that on that Monday morning she hurried out to Avellaneda across the trickle of the Riachuelo to see Cipriano Reyes, who, at Perón's request, had seized control of the meat packing house workers' union. She had a debt to collect, she told Reyes with blunt directness. The next morning, the first group of workers wended their way out of the Avellaneda slums, across the Riachuelo Bridge and into Buenos Aires. The new federal police chief had received orders to turn them back. But his men, whose sympathies were very much with Perón, did not work unduly hard at obeying the order. About 400 workers, mostly young men and teenagers, reached the city centre and began shouting for Perón. The police treated them leniently, limiting themselves most of the time to following them around with a tear gas squad. When the demonstrations threatened to get out of hand, the police intervened and broke them up with the use of a few tear gas bombs. But the workers quickly rallied and their shouts could be heard throughout the heart of the city all afternoon and late into the night.

The two generals and an admiral, who at the moment constituted all there was of a government in Argentina, had been meeting all morning in the Casa Rosada in an effort to find a political solution to the crisis which would be acceptable to all the various factions of the armed forces. From the president's window, they saw army officers being attacked on Plaza de Mayo by crowds shouting anti-Perón slogans. In the distance, they could hear chants of 'Viva Perón', growing louder as the day went by.

To Generals Farrell and Avalos, it seemed quite apparent that the military overthrow of Peron had somehow turned into a popular uprising against the army. Judging from what they had seen from the window. it had become open season on army officers. They decided there was only one solution if the army was to survive — Perón must be brought back. He should not be allowed to sit safely in a gaol cell while his fellow officers were being abused by the mob. Let him face the music. An official communiqué was issued from the Casa Rosada to the effect that Colonel Juan Perón was not, and never had been, under arrest. According to General Avalos, he had been taken to the naval prison on Martin Garcia Island under protective custody because his life had been threatened by undisciplined elements in the turmoil and excitement of the previous week's events.

It was a surprising statement, considering that the news of Perón's arrest had been published, with a wealth of detail by all Argentine newspapers, and that both General Avalos and Admiral Lima had taken credit for having put him under lock and key. Certainly no one was more surprised than Perón himself. He had been sitting in his cell, guarded by two sailors, when he heard his successor at the War Ministry on the radio blandly denying that he was under arrest. Perón had already written to Avalos demanding to be charged or set free. He had also asked to be moved to a Buenos Aires hospital because he said he was suffering from pleurisy. Both requests had been ignored. So this time he sent Avalos a telegram sarcastically suggesting that as he was not under arrest, his guards should be removed as he was quite capable of protecting himself. He received a reply at 3.30 in the morning of the 17th in the form of a police squad, which escorted him aboard a police launch, took him to the mainland, then drove him in an ambulance to the Central Military Hospital in Buenos Aires.

A strong military guard had cordoned off the hospital for three blocks in every direction. But that did not stop the workers who, in their thousands, streamed across the Riachuelo Bridge that morning. Most of them were coatless — a shocking sight in staid Buenos Aires where a man could go to jail for taking off his coat in a public park. Some had even discarded their shirts in the spring sunshine as they marched to the hospital, surrounded it, and set up a throbbing, repetitive cry of 'Pay-ron! Pay-ron!'

Throughout the day, workers continued to pour into Buenos Aires by bus and truck from the shanty slums — the villas miserias — on the outskirts, and, while the police stood passively by and the army held back, they took control of the city, singing, shouting slogans, and waving portraits of Peron. In the chaos, the middle-class porteños, who had gathered in Plaza San Martin only four days before, stayed at home behind shuttered windows; the General Confederation of Labour — Perón's umbrella organisation for all the unions — declared a general strike; and a delegation of workers was admitted to the military hospital and was received by one of Perón's leading henchmen, Colonel Domingo A. Mercante. Then, late in the afternoon, a tired, tight-lipped General Avalos pushed through the crowd outside the hospital entrance and went in to see Perón. They were together for over two hours, but what was said at that meeting has never been revealed. Afterwards, however, Avalos drove out to Campo de Mayo and resigned his army commission.

Within an hour of Avalos leaving the hospital, Perón and Eva were on their way to the Casa Rosada. In the car, she showed him a copy of an afternoon Buenos Aires newspaper which had printed pictures of the demonstrators, sneeringly titled: 'The shirtless ones (descamisados) who roam our streets.' Eva thrust the paper into his hands. 'There is your cause and your slogan,' she told him, her dark eyes blazing with excitement. When they arrived at the Presidential Palace, they found most of Perón's last cabinet (before his resignation) gathered there consulting with union delegations. President Farrell had already removed General Avalos and Admiral Lima from their ministerial posts. A new government was quickly formed with men totally loyal to Perón. He had left himself off the cabinet list as he had other plans. The vast crowd waiting noisily outside in the Plaza de Mayo certainly knew what they wanted for him. For the chant, louder than ever, was now, 'Perón for President.'

The throng beneath the balconies of the Casa Rosada had grown by the hour as thousands poured into the square from the cobbled dockside avenue below. There were perhaps 200,000 of them, most of them young, some of them were boys, but all of them obreros, working men with dark skins, rough hands, and cheap clothes. Perhaps they were the poorest of the poor. But they knew the name of the only man who had ever done anything for them. The chanted roar of 'Pay-ron' boomed on through the evening, hushing for a minute or two at eight o'clock as the windows leading to the main balcony of the palace were thrown open and it was announced that Perón would talk to the crowd within a few minutes. But, in fact, it was not until ten minutes past eleven that he appeared on the balcony with President Farrell. There was a great yell that lasted uninterrupted for ten minutes. The two men embraced, clasping each other around the shoulders. 'Here,' cried Farrell, 'is the man we all love — Juan Perón — the man who has conquered the hearts of all Argentines.'

Then Perón spoke. He told them he was ill and ailing, although his powerful, mesmeric voice showed no sign of weakness as it thundered across the packed plaza. He told them that he had resigned from the army. With a dramatic gesture, he unhooked his sword belt and handed it to President Farrell. 'I discard the honourable and sacred uniform of my country to put on the coat of the civil servant, and to mingle with the suffering and powerful masses which build up with their work the greatness of the nation. Herewith, I give my final adieu to the institution which is the fulcrum of the country: the army! I give, too, my first welcome to this huge crowd which represents the synthesis of a sentiment which seemed to have died in the Republic: the true civic status of the Argentine people!'

Then Perón remembered Eva's words. Holding out his arms to the crowd below, he roared: 'As a simple citizen, mingling with my descamisados, I wish to press all of you to my heart.' Behind him, in the great room of the Presidency, Eva smiled that smile of hers that curled up at the corner of her mouth. They were not yet shouting Evita — Little Eve. But that could wait. Her man was back in power. And she had put him there.

5

PERON FOR PRESIDENT

Buenos Aires, November 9 (AP) — A friend of Colonel Juan D. Perón said today that the former Vice-President of Argentina married Eva Duarte, a tall and attractive blonde, October 18. The informant, whose name may not be disclosed, said the marriage was performed in an apartment in Buenos Aires and that a Vital Statistics Bureau book was taken there to record the marriage.

It was the morning after Perón's triumphant return to power. The city was paralysed by a general strike. 'It would have been difficult to obtain even a glass of water in Buenos Aires,' grumbled the *New York Times'* correspondent, Arnaldo Cortesi, who also complained about the 'groups of irresponsible and rowdy young men who never seemed to tire of marching through the main thoroughfares shouting the name of Colonel Juan Perón as Buenos Aires lived through another day of mob rule.' Colonel J. Filomino Velazco had been reinstated as police chief. On the losing side, Admiral Hector Vernengo Lima — who had proudly proclaimed from the balcony of the Circulo Militar that 'I am not Perón. I am Admiral Vernengo Lima' — had fled the city with three units of Argentina's river squadron. He was threatened with severe measures, including the bombing of his ships from the air, if he did not return. This he finally decided to do and he was placed under arrest as soon as he reached Buenos Aires.

A triumphant Señora Maria Eva Duarte de Perón arrived back at the studios of Radio Belgrano to an effusive welcome from Jaime Yankelevich. He doubled her pay and dug even deeper into his pocket when she demanded restitution for the ten days she had been off the pay-roll. She was also making a film at the time, a major feature role in *The Spendthrift*, a production of one of Argentina's top film-makers, Miguel Marchiniendorena. He had already given her a leading role earlier in the year in a movie called *Circus Cavalcade*. The part had been promised to a much better known Argentine actress, Alita Roman. But Marchiniendorena was desperately trying to curry favour with Perón in an effort to get back the casino he had owned in Mar del Plata, which had been expropriated by the government.

Cavalcade did not help his cause at all. It was a disaster from start to finish. It starred Libertad Lamarque, who was still seething with rage at Eva for having stolen Perón right out of her arms at the charity concert at Luna Park a year earlier. Not being the most modest of young ladies, Eva flaunted her position as mistress of the nation's Strongman. She saw to it that Perón picked her up after work every day in his chauffeur-driven War Ministry limousine, and she behaved on the set as though she was the star, not Libertad. The inevitable explosion came when Eva sat in the chair which had Libertad's name on it. The star walked over and gave the younger woman a stinging slap across the face. With all that tension on the set, it was not surprising that the film was a box office disaster. Everybody agreed (though no one said so publicly) that Eva was terrible, a total failure as an actress. As for the lovely Libertad Lamarque, her films were banned in Argentina after October 17, 1945. She was forced into exile in Mexico City in order to make a living. She was one of many Argentines who were to discover that Eva Perón was totally unforgiving to her enemies.

Marchiniendorena certainly did not want to get on that list. So he gave Eva another chance in *Spendthrift*, the starring role this time. The male lead was Juan Jose Miguez, who had been responsible for Eva getting her very first job at Radio Belgrano. He had left radio work soon after that and had quickly established himself as a major star in Argentine movies, which in those days were mostly bad tear-jerkers. Miguez at first turned Eva down when she asked him to co-star with her in *Spendthrift*.

'Who was she to ask me to be her leading man?' he sniffed years later as he recalled the making of that movie. 'What was her background? At that time, she was living with Perón and could choose any play she wanted, cast, salary, everything. But I was quite frank about it. "You're mad at me," she said. "Of course," I replied. "If you were in my shoes you would feel that same way. At the moment I'm the biggest draw in Argentine movies. You've no experience at all. It would cheapen my standing to work with you." Those who heard me say this trembled for me. I added: "I don't want to stop you from acting. I just don't want to act with you." She got very angry. But we remained friends, and in the end, of course, I made the movie. It took six months to make, mainly because Eva was always having to take days off to go politicking. No one, of course, was going to fire her. And, as a matter of fact, we would have had problems making the movie without her. Film negative was scarce in those days. But I often saw Perón arriving on the set with several rolls of film under his arm. So we had to put up with her domineering everybody. She gave the orders, no doubt about that. But I'd argue with her so often that Mario Soficci, the director, would say to me: "Miguez, for God's sake stop contradicting her. You'll do it once too often." Actually, she was very good to me. She gave me ration coupons when petrol and tyres were rationed. On another occasion, she found out that I was short of money. She asked me what had happened and I finally confessed that I had taken some heavy gambling losses. She sent me 10,000 pesos (about £1,250 in those days) of her own money and never accepted repayment.'

So there was a soft spot in that tough, trim little figure. But those who saw it were mostly friends from the old days who had struggled as she had. Even poor, fat Jaime Yankelevich managed to survive, though he was constantly on the receiving end of the bruising side of her tongue. He kept on making errors of judgement that always cost him money in the form of salary rises for Eva. A couple of months after his expensive October miscalculation, he was approached by Eva with a demand to use the station to promote her husband's candidacy for president. He had formally thrown his hat in the ring on December 15 for the scheduled February 24 election. Jaime made some rapid calculations and got it wrong again. He said no. For a start all the knowledgeable political observers were convinced that Perón would get trounced in the election by the country's 'democrats' — radicals, conservatives, socialists, and even

53

communists. But more important than that, as far as Yankelevich was concerned, Perón had shown no visible signs of marrying his mistress.

For some reason, best known to themselves, the Peróns had not bothered to inform their countrymen that they had legalised their relationship. Maybe it was because Perón felt that, having humiliated his generals with his October 17 counter-revolution, he did not want to further embarrass them by upsetting their wives with a public announcement so soon afterwards that he had married his mistress. He knew that every wife on aristocratic Avenida Alvear would be aghast. 'That Woman' represented everything they hated and despised — the mistress who existed in almost every well-born Argentine man's life. If a man was so infatuated with his mistress that he married her, *they* would never accept her.

Eva, of course, did not mind how much she upset those particular ladies. But obviously she felt that her silence on this occasion was a small price to pay for her marriage certificate. But Jaime Yankelevich's refusal to allow Eva to use his radio station for presidential election campaigning — and the obvious reason for his refusal — were too much for her trigger-fast temper. 'You dirty Russian son-of-a-bitch,' she screamed. 'You'll see what happens if you refuse.' And as Jaime flinched, she brandished her marriage certificate under his nose. 'I tell you this as the First Lady of Argentina.' She was not. But she was too close for Yankelevich to dare argue about it.

As a matter of fact, the document was only a few days old. It was actually Eva's church marriage certificate. For although in law the Peróns had officially been married since their civil ceremony in October, in Catholic Argentina, it is really the church wedding that counts. Weddings to middle and upper-class Argentines conjure up images of white lace and sweet virgin brides. The thought of Eva Duarte — illegitimate, actress, mistress — marrying in church was to many of them sheer blasphemy. But in the early morning of December 9, three cars drew up to the Perón apartment building on Calle Posadas. A few minutes later, Colonel Perón, in army uniform despite his retirement, appeared at the front door arm-in-arm with Eva, who beamed a radiant smile under a fashionably floppy hat. She was wearing a simple white dress. They climbed into the back of Perón's Packard, and the convoy drove off to La Plata, the modern capital of the Province of Buenos Aires. There, in the cathedral, Juan Perón, widower, married Maria Eva Duarte, spinster. Her brother Juan gave her away, while Colonel Mercante, Perón's best friend who had just taken over the Labour Ministry in the new Farrell Government, served as his best man.

There was no time for a honeymoon. On the day before the wedding, the opposition Democratic Union, a coalition of parties opposed to Perón, held a campaign rally in Plaza del Congresso in downtown Buenos Aires. An estimated 200,000 porteños turned up for it. But they quickly learnt how dangerous it was to actively oppose Juan Perón. Gunmen opened fire on the crowd, which was then attacked by federal police. Four people were killed and 35 injured. The following Friday, Perón appeared in public for the first time since his October 17 come-back, presenting himself as the presidential candidate of his own political party, the Labour party, which he had formed specially to represent the descamisados who had taken the city by storm on that October day. Between 100,000 and 150,000 people once again flooded the centre of the city to see their hero take his place on a floodlit platform at the foot of a towering, needle-shaped obelisk that stands in the middle of Avenida Nueve de Julio, which Argentines justifiably claim as the world's widest avenue.

To ensure that Perón's enemies could not revenge themselves for the previous week's killings in Plaza de Congresso, federal police took elaborate precautions. Mounted, motorised and foot police, reinforced by riot and tear gas squads, patrolled the streets in great numbers. People going to the meeting had to pass through a triple cordon of police. All the buildings in the vicinity were searched, and police with rifles were posted on the rooftops. The owners of the houses facing Avenida Nueve de Julio, all of them certainly middle and upper class, were warned by police that they would be held responsible for the behaviour of people watching from their windows or balconies. But there was no trouble at. It was a happy, noisy crowd that cheered so loudly when Perón appeared on the platform with his tiny, slender wife that it was almost fifteen minutes before he could be heard.

His voice boomed out over the loudspeakers down the wide avenue, rolling over the swaying, banner-waving mass of humanity. 'Consolidating our future, I join the ranks of the descamisados,' he cried, taking off his coat and rolling up the sleeves of his white shirt to bare his hairy forearms. That was exactly the sort of thing his descamisados had come out of the

55

slums to hear. They roared their appreciation, a roar that faded to a gentle hum as Perón explained his plans for their future. He promised, if elected, to give them shorter working hours, a share in their company's profits, state-built housing, and, under the leadership of his wife, political rights for women, who had never had any in Argentina.

It was revolutionary stuff by Argentine standards. Politicians had never campaigned for the working class vote before. They did not have to. Elections in the past were always stolen by the Conservatives with stuffed ballot boxes except during the brief period of middle-class Radical Party government in the 1920s. But now here was a man who not only promised to look after the country's working class people but who, during his period at the Labour Ministry, had already done more for them than anyone ever had. He was their man, and the admiration was mutual. As the hour grew late and Perón's long oration finally came to an end, he and his wife slowly waved an Argentine flag from whose pole hung a sweaty workman's shirt. From the vast crowd in front of them came the thundered response of 'Pay-ron! Pay-ron!'

That chanted name became a battle-cry during the next ten weeks of the campaign. For many Argentines it was a sound to be dreaded. With the army and federal police openly showing support for Perón, there was no protection for his opponents or their supporters. Violent disorders were almost a daily occurrence as packs of pro-Perón thugs roamed the capital. The city's Jews — 400,000 of them, the largest Jewish community in South America — were one of their favourite targets, news which sent chills around a world still digesting the horrors of Buchenwald. 'Kill a Jew and be a patriot,' was just one of many anti-Semitic slogans splashed in red paint on the walls of the Jewish quarter of the city. After one pro-Perón demonstration, crowds of young Perónistas invaded the quarter to loot Jewish-owned shops, brutally beating anyone who attempted to stop them. In scenes reminiscent of Nazi Germany in the 1930s, police stood by while Jews were knocked to the ground and kicked. When the police did act, it was usually to arrest the victims.

'Alarm and even terror are beginning to spread in the Jewish quarter,' reported the New York Times' Cortesi, adding that 'It is hardly possible to doubt any longer that anti-semitism forms part of Colonel Perón's political stock in trade.' Certainly the attacks on the country's Jewish population could not have happened without Perón's tacit approval. As the country's Strongman, he could put a stop to it at any time. Eventually he did. Perhaps it finally dawned on him that his country stood in danger of being labelled the international pariah of the post-war world. So before the end of December, he publicly condemned those supporters of his who had taken part in attacks on Jews. 'Those doing so,' he said, 'are outside all democratic standards and cannot be regular members of any Argentine political force.'

But Perón's dispensation to Argentina's Jews did not extend to his other political opponents. Throughout January 1946, the streets of Buenos Aires were constantly blotted out by billows of tear gas as police moved in to break up battles between warring factions in which Perón's opponents almost always came off second best. The reason why was simply explained by the Assistant Inspector of the federal police, Alejandro Jorge Gallardo, when he resigned in disgust over the behaviour of his colleagues. In his letter of resignation he wrote: 'In the streets of Buenos Aires and several towns of the interior, I have witnessed Perónista gangs of hoodlums attacking our women and mistreating our brethren while counting on the passiveness of officials charged with keeping order.' But Gallardo's gesture achieved nothing. The harassment continued.

When the Democratic Union's Presidential candidate, Dr Jose P. Tamborini, and Vice-Presidential candidate, Dr Enrique M. Mosca, set off on a whistle-stop campaign tour of the interior late in January, the train was repeatedly stoned as it steamed through the countryside. Wherever it stopped, the candidates' meetings were almost invariably broken up by small bands of Perónistas while police stood idly by. In Entre Rios, the province immediately to the north of Buenos Aires, federal officials banned all public meetings and allowed the train to halt only for re-fuelling. Not until after it had been set on fire, a small boy killed, and the candidates' campaign literature destroyed, did the Government order 50 armed soldiers to ride shot-gun on the train to prevent any further violence. In Cordoba, the largest city in the interior, Tamborini told a sympathetic audience that he wanted to 'remove from Argentine public life this impudence which sells the public offices of the state as electoral arsenals, which converts them into recruiting offices for street rioters. We desire order, peace, the ability to live together, and respect for law.'

Dr Tamborini was hoping for too much in the emotion-charged atmosphere of Argentina's first real presidential election campaign in sixteen years. When his rock-gashed train arrived back in Buenos Aires, police fired on the crowd that had gathered to greet him in the Plaza Once outside the station. Three young men were killed and many others wounded. Explaining away the gunfire on people whose only crime had been that some of them had started chanting, 'to the gallows with Perón', police said they had done so to restore order.

But the dirty tricks were not totally one-sided. In fact, Perón and Eva came close to serious injury, possibly death, during one of their trips to the interior. Their train jumped the tracks just after midnight on February 10, as they were leaving Rosario, the granary city of Argentina, on their journey back to the capital. It was discovered that the axle of the rear coach had been neatly sawn to the point where it was bound to break sooner or later with the swaying of the moving train. All that saved those aboard from disaster was that the train was travelling slowly instead of its normal 40 to 60 miles an hour when the axle finally did go. Perón and Eva were eating in the dining car when the brakes were jammed on, the whistle shrieked, and the coach bucked wildly. Fearing an ambush, the Peróns' bodyguards, armed with sub-machine guns, jumped off and disappered into the darkness. Everybody on the coach, except for the Peróns, flung themselves on the floor. But Juan Perón gripped his wife's hand across the table, grinned at her, and then told everybody not to be so foolish and get back to their seats. The damage was minor and the train was soon on its way again.

Apart from that incident, the trip had been a dazzling success. A large, enthusiastic crowd had seen the train off from Retiro Station in Buenos Aires after youngsters swarmed all over it, chalking campaign slogans on the coaches and roofs. As it steamed slowly across the pampas towards Rosario, it passed waving, cheering groups of country people at every small station and farm along the route. Most of them were young, farm workers, their wives and children, the women shrieking, the men waving their shirts, some even chasing the train, grabbing the rail of the guard's coach at the back and running with it for a few yards. In Rosario, industrial labourers crushed each other in the mad scramble to touch Juan and Eva's hands through the coach window as the train eased to a halt. Secret police protecting the candidate and his wife hauled a fainting woman through the window at Perón's command and Eva helped to give her first aid while the Rosario police battled to clear a path so that the two of them could leave the train.

It was a stiflingly hot and humid summer's night with the huge, sweating crowd packed tight into the city's main plaza. Women and children fainted by the hundreds. Gauchos in their baggy *bombacha* trousers, flowing shirts and high-brimmed hats sat astride their horses in the throng, singing Perónista songs. Swarms of locusts blanketed the night sky, clinging to clothes and faces, crunching beneath thousands of feet, adding their own peculiar stench to the sweat of the people. Palm trees and banana trees in the square swayed with the weight of young men and children. Every viewing point, from lamp-posts to narrow ledges on the sides of all the buildings facing the square, was occupied. Thousands more unable to fight their way into the plaza stood in the side streets listening to the speeches booming out over the loudspeakers. Encircled by a company of armed sailors, the Peróns slowly edged their way to the speakers' platform. Now, for the first time, the chanting had a double-barrelled sound to it, not just 'Pay-ron' but 'Pay-ron, Ay-vita.'

Eva did not speak that night. But the women in the crowd in the plaza and along the side of the railway tracks gaped and sighed in pleasure at the sight of the lovely young blonde in her beautiful clothes and jewellery who stood with such commanding assurance at the side of their hero. Perón only spoke for half an hour. But that did not matter. It was the event that counted, that people who led such brutally impoverished and barren lives could actually see, and some could even touch, the man who was not only promising but actually bringing them a better life. On the six-hour journey home to Buenos Aires in the dawn light, teen-age girls ran in relays alongside the train together with whooping gauchos whose galloping horses raised clouds of yellow dust that blotted out the flat plains of the pampas. As the train crawled into the capital, the crowds thickened, arms outstretched in supplication.

Jose Tamborini could never match that kind of adulation. He was a plump, little man, 60 years old, honest and uninspiring, a Radical politician in Congress since 1918. He was then young and vigorous and bursting with the ideals and dreams of the middle-class Radical revolution. Now he was rather elderly, not very radical, and rather tired, bewildered and not a little frightened by the tumultuous, angry tempo of the election. His support ranged from Communist to Conservative, and, inevitably, with that odd melange, the Democratic Union campaign focused on what it was against rather than what it was for, and what it was against was Juan Perón, fiend incarnate to

59

all those Argentines who were not convinced Perónistas.

But even those whose hatred of him never wavered admitted that he had all the charisma. He was good-looking, had a nimble wit, a ready smile, could talk in the slang of the city *barrios* or the dialect of the provinces, ate his barbecued beef with a razor-sharp knife like the gauchos, and was always ready to while away an evening in a dockside bar, drinking raw wine and swapping jokes. And he could tap the emotions with the skill of an orchestral conductor, rousing crowds to patriotic fervour one minute, then hushing them to silence, the tears streaming down his face as he talked about his dear mother. But to most political observers and to all the foreign correspondents in Buenos Aires for the election, such demagoguery, as they called it, could not survive a secret ballot box election. Tamborini, the democrat, was a firm favourite to beat Perón, the fascist dictator. On the eve of the vote, Cortesi wrote in the *New York Times*: 'All that can be said is that the turnout for the opposition candidate in most of the large cities visited by both indicates that the Democratic Union should triumph if tomorrow's election is even approximately fair and honest.'

Perón went down with the flu on election day, February 24, with Eva acting as his nurse in their Calle Posadas apartment. But they both managed to get to the local polling station, and then he went back to bed. The city was as quiet as a cemetery. All the bars were shuttered as were the theatres and cinemas. The Buenos Aires commuter trains, normally packed to bursting, ran virtually empty throughout the day. Long lines waited patiently outside the polling stations from early morning until the polls closed. There were no incidents. With the ugly campaign over — more than 100 people had been killed — Argentines voted peaceably and democratically for a President for the first time in many years. Troops with fixed bayonets escorted the ballot boxes to the national Congress building in Buenos Aires and to the provincial capitals in the interior. But the counting did not begin until March 6.

First, the ballot boxes were checked to make sure they had not been tampered with, and Argentines also took time off for the annual celebration of Carnival. Then, under the eye of delegates from both parties, the counting began. On March 28, it was announced that Juan Domingo Perón had been elected President of Argentina for a six-year term. In voting terms, it had been fairly close — 1,527,231 to 1,207,155. But even so, it was a nation-wide victory of overwhelming proportions. Perón won the Governorships of all 15 provinces, all 30 Senate seats and an overwhelming majority in the lower house of Congress with 109 deputies to 49. In Avellaneda, where the revolution of October 17 began, Perón won a lop-sided 68 percent of the votes. Even the city of Buenos Aires with its large middle-class gave him 54 percent of the votes.

The Peróns won not simply because he was a demagogue and she controlled the country's major radio stations but because they did the job that their democratic opponents should have been doing — going to the people with a programme of economic justice. In the rural provinces of the interior, Perón chalked up sweeping victories among peasants whose lives were brutish and short, where infant mortality rates were high, and disease — malaria, tapeworm, tuberculosis, goitre, influenza — and malnutrition had bred generation after generation of anaemic, impoverished people. Even in the country's capital, a private medical study had shown that 30,000 Buenos Aires children did not attend school because of malnutrition. Perón also addressed himself to the fact that half of Buenos Aires' workers' families lived in one room. He also stressed and promised to remedy the inequitable system of Argentine land-holding — two thousand landlords owning the richest fifth of the land while 70 percent of the farms were run by sharecroppers who paid half their income out in rent.

In the last few days of the campaign, Perón was handed an election issue which had nothing to do at all with economics or social justice. To his delight, the United States took that particular moment to add yet another chapter to its unhappy record of Big Stick diplomacy in Latin America. The State Department, in a move to influence the election, published a handbook reviewing Perón's record of fascism and collaboration with Nazi Germany in World War II. Primly titled *Consultation among the American Republics with Respect to the Argentine Situation*, but better known as the 'Blue Book', it was the work of Assistant Secretary of State Spruille Braden, whose brief ambassadorship in Buenos Aires the previous year had been marked by the blunt, undiplomatic manner with which he had publicly attacked Perón and the Argentine Government. Braden was determined to stamp out the vestiges of Nazism in the southern continent, even though Nazism had already been replaced by Communism in the American mind as the enemy of world peace and democracy.

The other Latin American nations recognised the 'Blue Book'

for what it was — an attempt by the Americans to go on fighting a war that was over — and they ignored it. Perón and many Argentines, not all of them Perón supporters, looked upon it as unacceptable meddling in their country's internal affairs. Eva quickly took advantage of such a marvellous propaganda gift for those final days of the campaign. In her radio broadcasts, which went out to every town and village in the country, she called on all Argentines to repudiate the threat of 'Yanqui' imperialism with the cry of 'Perón yes! Braden no!' It was an unbeatable slogan and almost certainly won the votes of many indignant patriotic Argentines who would otherwise have voted for Tamborini.

However, Perón himself felt that the election had been won long before the American intervention. Like others, he recognised that the campaign until then had been entirely, for or against him. As he put it, 'the opposition shouts "Death to Perón". My supporters shout "Long Live Perón". We are for a better life, and they are for a moribund one. Those two words — "muera" and "viva" — symbolise the difference.'

On June 4, 1946, Juan Domingo Perón became the twenty-ninth President of Argentina. Restored to his army commission and promoted, he wore the blue dress uniform of a brigadier-general as he stood before the newly reconstituted Congress and took the oath of office, swearing by 'Almighty God' to uphold the constitution. Exactly three years to the day after his band of colonels seized the Government, he pledged 'respect for the country's traditions and institutions.' Then, to the notes of martial music and the cheers of a million Argentines, he drove along Avenida de Mayo to the Casa Rosada.

Never in Argentine history had there been such tumultuous crowds. Police and troops tried desperately to keep the cheering mob from sweeping over the presidential limousine. But it took over an hour to make what would normally be a five minute journey to the palace. There, in the White Salon, grenadiers in uniforms dating from the time of Napoleon — red pompon-topped shakos with gold chin-straps, red and gold epaulets, and white cross belts on blue tunics with red-striped trousers — lined the walls of the magnificent state room. Under a huge chandelier, whose light was reflected from gold ornamentation on ceilings, cornices, and doors, the room dazzled with the plumage of diplomats, high-ranking military officers, and their wives. British scarlet blended with the purple of two Cardinals. Rows of medals gleamed from the breasts of multi-coloured uniforms. General Farrell, like President Perón, wore a dark blue uniform with the broad blue and white sash of the presidency across his chest. The transfer of power took only three minutes. General Farrell handed President Perón a mace resembling a marshal's baton and then placed the colours of office across his friend's shoulders. 'I wish you personal success and success for your new administration,' General Farrell said, with tears streaming down his face. The two men embraced. Beside the President stood Argentina's new First Lady, Señora Maria Eva Duarte de Perón.

6

EVITA — FIRST LADY

Argentines, among the most socially conservative of all Latins, had never seen anything like it. For them, a lady's place — and that went for the First Lady — was in the home. But from the moment of the inauguration, Eva Perón changed all that. She encouraged the public to call her Evita in a land where nicknames are restricted to the closest friends. Larger than life pictures of the country's First Lady blossomed all over the country, carrying her words: 'I prefer to be simply Evita if this Evita is used to better conditions in the homes of my country.' Her own home, once an adobe shack in the poorest of rural pueblos, was now the most luxurious residence in the country — the old Palacio Unzue on fashionable Avenida Alvear. It looked out across the wide avenue towards the trees of Palermo Park and the river beyond. Furnished in sombre, ornate nineteenth-century style, its manicured lawns and flower beds of blue jacaranda and magnolias provided an oasis of tranquillity in the heart of the noisy, bustling city.

The Peróns lived there rather than in the more traditional presidential residence in suburban Olivos because they both worked a brutally demanding dawn-to-dark routine. Up at 6am, breakfast together at 6.30, then Eva was off to work with an escort of police motorcyclists, sirens wailing to clear the way and wake her wealthy neighbours on the avenue. In her sumptuously furnished office on the fourth floor of the Central Post Office, surrounded by a battery of secretaries, she would spend her mornings receiving delegations of workers and trade unionists, who came from every corner of the land to pay their respects, and, more often than not, seek her support for a wage claim. Nurses and teachers joined the throng, eager to hear the views of the nations's foremost feminist, who promised to liberate Argentina's women from the shackles of their *macho* society. Senators, congressmen, mayors, even Cabinet Ministers rubbed shoulders in the corridors, waiting their turn to push a cause or seek a favour.

After a quick lunch back at the residence with the General, she was off again, visiting factories, schools, slum neighbourhoods, flying off on quick trips to rally the Perónista faithful in distant towns. Among her duties, she took over the president's traditional role of acting as a godparent for all seventh sons, in recognition of the family's contribution to the country's much-needed population growth. Evita, of course, always made sure that her godmotherly missions received nation-wide publicity. Before the baptismal ceremony of a seventh son in Avellaneda, trucks equipped with loudspeakers announced her presence and urged the local meat packing house workers, her descamisados, and their families to turn up in force. The lucky family would receive a new home; a gift from Evita. For the neighbours, there were clothes, shoes, toys, schoolbooks, and even peso notes.

Not surprisingly, wherever Evita went the crowds scrambled and fought to get close to her. When she travelled to Tucuman Province in the north-west of the country, where the sugar workers lived in abject poverty, seven people were crushed to death in the rush for gifts, which were always accompanied by a pep talk that could be guaranteed to be full of rousing melodrama.

In Tucuman, the death of the seven sugar workers prompted her to cry out that 'I, too, like our companion workers, am capable of dying and of ending the last moment of my life with our war cry, our cry of salvation, "my life for Perón".' On another occasion, she promised her audience that 'embracing the patria, I will give my all, because there are as yet in this country those who are poor and unhappy, without hope and sick. My soul knows it. My body has felt it. I offer all my energies that my body may be stretched out like a bridge towards the common happiness. Cross over it with a firm tread and head high towards the supreme destiny of our new patria. Not fatigue, nor fasting, nor sacrifice can be of importance when you are trying to put an end to the fatigue and suffering that dwell in the country's organs.

Understandably, sophisticated Argentines shuddered when they heard such emotional rhetoric. But it was not easy to avoid. Not only were her sayings splashed across the nation on billboards, it was impossible to turn on a radio anywhere in Argentina without being bombarded by the thoughts of Evita on just about everything from tips to combat inflation to lessons on the duties and privileges of citizenship, which were always accompanied with constant reminders that all the wonderful things happening in Argentina were being brought about through the devotion and idealism of their beloved leader, President Perón. Those nightly fireside chats were carried live by the state radio network, and local radio stations throughout the country were forced to hook in by order of the director of the Department of Posts and Telegraph, Oscar Nicolini, who worked in the next office to Evita under her direct supervision. Just what some Argentines thought of their president's wife and her pearls of wisdom they kept to the privacy of their cocktail parties, although bawdy limericks about her soon began to appear on walls around the city.

Evita was not particularly concerned about what the wealthy, the oligarchs as she contemptuously called them, felt about her. Even without the sniggering, she had a lot of old scores to settle with them, scores that went back to her earliest childhood memories, and she intended to settle them. As a matter of fact, she felt quite confident that the matrons of porteña society would be forced to accept her whether they liked it or not — and she knew perfectly well they did not. She intended to claim all the social honours normally bestowed on the president's wife in Argentina. So, throughout most of her first year in the Casa Rosada, she waited impatiently to be offered the traditional presidency of the Sociedad de Beneficiencia, the country's most exclusive charitable organisation, run by the ladies of Argentine society under the patronage of the Catholic Church. It never came.

But Evita was not the kind of person to ignore such a snub. She sent an emissary to the society's organising committee to enquire why she had not heard from them. With the smoothness and charm that distinguishes the well-bred South American, the ladies responded that, alas, she was too young, the rules of the charity required a woman of more mature years as its leader.

67

With equal silkiness, Evita then suggested that they should make her mother Dona Juana, president. The thought of that plump, little peasant woman, who could hardly read or write, who had given birth to five illegitimate children, as their president may or may not have amused the good ladies. But the answer was the same — no. From then on it was total, constant war. In her fury, Evita set about destroying the society women and their organisation.

But first she still had some organising of her own to do. She began putting her family in positions of power. Her brother, Juancito, she placed in the Casa Rosada as her husband's private secretary, controlling all access to the President, quite a sudden rise in fortunes for a not particularly successful Junin soap salesman. But then Evita was very fond of her big brother. He was a handsome young man in the Argentine mold of the period — jet black hair greased back and pencil-thin moustache — and he soon became well known around Buenos Aires as an escort of the prettiest girls in town. Evita was always having to rescue him from financial and emotional scrapes. But now she had a use for him — to make sure that no one got to the ear of her husband without her knowing about it. As for the rest of the family, she promoted her mother's friend, Oscar Nicolini, to Minister of Communications. Eldest sister Elisa took over political control of Junin while her husband, Major Alfredo Arrieto, was elected through Evita's influence to the Senate. Sister Blanca's husband, Dr Justo Alvarez Rodriguez, a lawyer, became in quick succession the Governor of Buenos Aires Province, a key position as the province contained over half the country's population, and then a member of the Supreme Court. Even Arminda's husband did well. He was the lift operator in the town hall at Junin. But one push of the button from Evita and he was on his way up to Director of Federal Customs.

Evita did not forget herself. She moved her office from the Central Post Office to her husband's old stamping ground, the Ministry of Labour and Social Welfare. Taking over the management of the descamisados, the linch-pin of Perón's power, she quickly won their love with mammoth pay increases. She was not the Secretary of Labour — in fact, she never held any post in the Government, elected or appointed — not that it mattered. Jose Maria Freire, a glassblower by profession, who was Labour Secretary, soon found himself shunted aside. When the railway workers called and asked for a 40 percent rise, Evita offered them 50 percent. Then the telephone workers put in a request for 70 per cent, hoping for half, but collecting the lot. Understandably, there was soon hardly a single union left outside the protective embrace of Perón's General Confederation of Labour (the CGT) as workers discovered that pay raises went to those unions which did as Evita suggested. Before long, over five million of the country's seven million-strong labour force had joined the CGT. The crowds that gathered in Plaza de Mayo in front of the presidential palace now cried Evita's name with every bit as much fervour as they did her husband's. And it was her voice which reverberated through the loudspeakers and around the plaza with the message that she was just 'one more descamisada, the most insignificant of General Perón's collaborators.'

The General did not think so. He confided to a friend that 'Evita deserves a medal for what she's done for labour. She's worth more to me than five Ministers.' Of course, he had not been entirely idle himself during those first few months in office. On his first day, he arrived at the Casa Rosada at 7am, surprising employees who were accustomed to the leisurely habits of former presidents. But even before he put on the sash of office he had begun making revolutionary changes.

By decree, the Government seized control of the six great Argentine universities, putting in its own Rectors and ordering an end to student political activity on the pain of expulsion. The banks were taken over. So was the Buenos Aires Stock Exchange — all first tugs on the noose that slowly had begun to snuff out individual freedom in Argentina but carried out within the legalistic framework of constitutional government.

The federal bureaucracy was put under close scrutiny. Everyone 'not imbued with the revolutionary ideals or imbued with the precepts of social justice' soon found themselves without a job. Perón also settled an old score with the Rural Society, the organisation and stronghold of the landed aristocracy. His name had been booed the previous year at the society's internationally-famed cattle show. Now, as the nation's president, it was his duty to turn up in top hat and tails to open the show, and he was determined to be cheered, not booed. So, under pressure, the society's executive committee obligingly resigned and a pro-Perón committee was appointed.

At the same time, he moved against a much more important target — the nation's Supreme Court. Perón had scores to settle there, too. During his period as Secretary of Labour, the court had overturned a number of his labour and welfare decrees on the grounds that they were unconstitutional, and it had also released several army officers and federal judges who had been thrown in jail by Perón. So, naturally, when the Strongman was briefly toppled from power in the turbulent October days of 1945, many Argentines turned to the Supreme Court with the suggestion that it take over the reigns of government on a temporary basis. But as the generals and admirals argued, Perón vaulted back into the saddle before the move could be made. However, he did not forget what might have been. In his inaugural address, he made it clear that the judges would have to pay for their emnity.

'I place the spirit of justice above the judicial power,' he warned, adding that the court did not 'speak the same language as the other branches of the government.' Within days, the Perónista-controlled Congress set out to impeach the entire Supreme Court. With fine irony, the judges were charged with having betrayed their office by recognising the regime that had been set up by Perón's colonels in June of 1943. The chief justice resigned but all four other justices were duly impeached. They, and other judges throughout the country, were replaced by lawyers willing to allow the judiciary to be as completely controlled by Juan and Evita Perón as the other branches of Government. As Chief Justice Roberto Repetto left office he warned his fellow countrymen that 'a new state power has been instituted above the constitution and above the law. This power has risen on the ruins of public liberties.'

But those Argentines who listened were in no position to do anything about it. The only power that could possibly have done so was the army, and Perón saw to it that the army stayed in line with lavish wage increases for officers and men. Indeed, most of Argentina's 16 million population was living better than ever as their country prospered from a war-ravaged world's desperate need for its wheat and beef. Perón certainly showed no compunction in holding up hungry nations to ransom. 'Either you pay our prices or you don't eat,' was the blunt, initial negotiation remark of his economic czar, Miguel Miranda, when he first met a British commercial mission that had arrived in Buenos Aires to arrange a new trade agreement. The British, who were Argentina's oldest and best customers, were told they would have to pay a 200 per cent increase in price if they wanted Argentine's meat. The United Nation's Relief Agency, responsible in those early post-war days for feeding much of starving Europe, was also told that it would not get its promised wheat, corn, and linseed oil until it paid an extra 100 per cent on the purchase price.

As for the Americans, the wily Perón had already seen advantages for Argentina in the fast-growing cold war between the US and the Soviet Union. So when the State Department pressed its demand that Argentina hand over the top 100 Nazis who had fled there at the end of the war, Perón curtly refused, remarking that he would just as soon as do business with the Russians if the US continued that kind of pressure. To drive the point home, he had the Russian trade delegation seated prominently at his inauguration, while his descamisados vociferously booed the American ambassador and the US delegation. Later, Perón gleefully told an Argentine banker, 'You'll see, the Americans will soon be down here with satchels looking for business.'

He was quite right. American President Harry S. Truman sent a new ambassador to Buenos Aires, James Bruce, with instructions to 'go down there and make friends with those people.' Right behind the flag swarmed the American business-men just as Perón had predicted. In fact, one of the first big business deals, put together by a Cleveland company, was with an Argentine-German industrialist named Ricardo Staudt, who had been the number two Nazi in the State Department's 'Blue Book'. The American company's comment about that was 'the war is over and finished.' But despite American overtures, Perón never missed an opportunity to make it clear that Argentina had no intention of becoming an ally of the 'Colossus of the North' in its cold war with the Soviet Union.

Defining his country's 'Third Position', Perón stated: 'There is in the world at the present time a conflict between capitalists and communists and we do not wish to be one thing or the other;' and on another occasion: 'We will not defend capitalism, in fact, we are dismantling it bit by bit.' That was not exactly true. But Perón was dismantling foreign capitalist control over Argentina's economy, a revolutionary and immensely popular move in a country where foreigners controlled close to 60 percent of all industrial investment, and where a third of all profits earned from the sweat of Argentine brows disappeared overseas in the form of dividends.

The British were the main targets for Perón's economic revolution. They controlled two-thirds of all foreign investment in Argentina. They owned nearly all the public utilities — the Americans had the rest — and they held a virtual stranglehold

71

on the economy through their domination of the meat packing industry, shipping, banking, and insurance. One story, no doubt apocryphal, which could always be guaranteed to drive an Argentine nationalist to fury concerned the Duke of Windsor when he was Prince of Wales. A frequent visitor to the British-owned estancias and polo fields of Argentina, he was reputed to have joked on returning to England after one such trip that 'I don't mind what part of the Empire we give up as long as it isn't Argentina.'

Perón was detemined to wipe that colonialist smirk from British faces. To underline his determination, he travelled to Tucuman, a provincial city in the heart of Argentina where in 1816 General Jose de San Martin, the nation's George Washington, fathered the formal proclamation of Argentine independence. On the same spot, Perón signed the 'declaration of economic independence', promising the Argentine people that he would 'break the dominating chains which have bound them to foreign captialism.' Evita added her own endorsement to that with a warning to foreign governments who might try and prevent the loss of their investments that 'the days have passed when our destinies can be settled thousands of miles from our shores; today we Argentines are the architects of our own destiny.'

Soon enough, the gasworks, the electricity companies, the telephone system — all British or American owned — were in Argentine hands, bought with the fat profits from the sale of the country's meat and grain. But what the Peróns wanted most of all were the railways, the most conspicuous example of the country's colonial economic status. All Argentines rode on them to get anywhere in the vast spaces of their land, and nearly all of Argentina's rich agricultural produce moved by rail. Yet this vital sector of the nation's economy had been neglected and allowed to run down for years. There were 27,000 miles of track, owned by nine different British companies, and Perón was determined to make every last mile of it Argentine, as Britain's trading mission quickly discovered when they arrived to buy meat. The British were in no position to pay Argentina the £190 million they still owed for wartime meat purchases. So Perón simply wiped £150 million from the British debt and took over the railways.

For Argentina, it was a day of celebration with patriotic ceremonies, speeches, and firework displays in plazas large and

Evita with her lover a year before their marriage.

The young marrieds in 1946 at their country *quinta* outside Buenos Aires.

Evita distributing gifts to her *descamisados* on a whistle-stop tour into the interior provinces.

On the balcony of the Casa Rosada, Evita and Perón greet the cheering crowds in the plaza below.

A glance of love and affection on a formal occasion.

The Rainbow Tour: On a Madrid street with Señora Franco.

Above: Arriving in Rome, brother Juancito by her side.

Below: With President Franco and the matadors.

small across the nation. In Buenos Aires, church bells, factory whistles, and train sirens pealed and hooted noisily throughout the day and evening. The architects of everybody's joy, however, were missing from the celebrations. Perón had been operated on the day before for emergency appendicitis. But he was not one to miss any opportunity to take a bow, even from a hospital bed. In a husky voice, carried by radio and loudspeakers to a vast crowd gathered outside Retiro, the main Buenos Aires railway station, he told his countrymen how happy he was that the railways were theirs. A few seconds later another now familiar voice surged over the airwaves. 'Comrade Evita was also unable to be with you today because she had to stay at the bedside of the *lider* of the workers. But you can be sure that both the General and I were with you from here because our heart is permanently at the side of our beloved descamisados who are really forging the greatness of our country. Descamisados mios: I send you an affectionate embrace.'

They made a good team. While Perón handled the diplomats, the politicians and businessmen, Evita looked after the voters who brought them to power — her descamisados. The country's Indians, so abused in the past, were the first to seek her help. Several hundred of them marched into Buenos Aires after a 1,000 mile trek across the pampas from the sugar fields in the north. They represented some 75,000 Indians living on the fringes of white Argentina. Their ancestors, unlike the fierce araucanian Indians of the pampas, were peaceful farmers who had been quickly absorbed by Spanish colonists for use as labourers in the fields. They no longer even owned the land they lived on. It had been sold by shrewd land dealers to absentee landlords at the turn of the century. Now the owners were trying to move the Indians out.

The evictions, accompanied by the burning of homes and even bloodshed where the resistance was violent, provided Evita with an opportunity to dramatise the sincerity of one of her vote-catching slogans — 'the land belongs to him who works it.' So she inspired the march, telling the Indians when she spoke to them from the balcony of the Casa Rosada that the government had stopped the evictions and was in the process of passing new laws that would make the land theirs again. For the landowners those Argentines who had for so long treated the country as one vast estancia, their worst fears about *that* woman were already being realised. But to the Indians and to all Argentine's rural workers, Evita's words were proof enough that her promises made were promises kept.

However, she wielded a hatchet with the same dexterity that she waved her angel's wand. Even the most senior of Peronista politicians found out that to cross the 27-year-old wife of the president was tantamount to committing political suicide. The first to learn that painful lesson was the head of the Peronista majority in the Senate, Vicente Eli Saadi. He was the son of Syrian immigrants, a true descamisado who had shot up through the ranks of provincial Peronistas via a combination of intelligence, charm, and good looks. But that jump from local Deputy in rural Catamarca to running the upper house of the national Congress must have gone to young Saadi's head. For he could not possibly have been thinking properly the day he rose during a closed session of the Senate to object to the presence of an 'outsider.' The outsider, of course, was Evita. She just smiled, apologised for her error, and left.

A few days later, Senator Saadi was called in to the Casa Rosada, where the President and his wife congratulated him on having been chosen personally by them as the strongest possible candidate to run for Governor of Catamarca Province. As modesty was not one of the Senator's best-known qualities, he saw no reason to quarrel with that assessment. So he left his Senate seat, returned home and easily won election as Governor. But it was not long before he started hearing rumours from the capital suggesting that he was under investigation for corruption, an investigation ordered by Evita Perón. The word was that he could expect to be removed from office any day. With that knowledge, Saadi came up with an astute ploy to save himself. He assembled his legislature, submitted his resignation as Governor, then had the deputies re-elect him to his old seat in the Senate, where he guessed it would be too politically embarrassing for the Peróns to remove him. But Evita was too quick for him, as she was for all her enemies. She persuaded her husband to 'intervene' in the Province of Catamarca, which meant putting it under federal control and dismissing both the Governor and his legislature. The intervention was back-dated 24 hours prior to Saadi's resignation. Immediately afterwards, he was thrown out of the Peronista Party and then jailed for showing disrespect to the president.

Evita's enemies had a way of disappearing like that. Her memory was a long one for past insults, real or imagined. As her General too liked to play the the role of the goodhearted, lovable uncle, she took care of his enemies with equal gusto.

74

When she could not jail them, she harassed them, often making life so miserable that many fled across the river to the tranquillity of neighbouring Uruguay.

One of their most vocal critics in those early days was one of the country's leading academics, Dr Bernardo Houssay. He had been jailed briefly during the purge of opponents the previous September, and after the presidential election he became one of the many hundreds of anti-Perón educators ousted from university posts. But then, much to the Government's embarrassment, he won the Nobel Prize for Medicine. Evita was furious, livid with rage, the more so as the Perónista press for weeks had been campaigning for the award of the Nobel Peace Prize for her husband. So, despite the fact that the award was undoubtedly an historic honour for both Argentine medicine and the nation, the Perónist press embarked on a venomous campaign of personal abuse against Dr Houssay, whom *La Epoca*, one of the most strident of the papers, called 'that gland detective'.

Such vindictiveness caused no concern to ordinary working class Argentines. They worshipped Evita because for the first time they were winning the praise and the awards. When Delfo Cabrero, a Buenos Aires fireman, won the Olympic marathon in London, he wired home dedicating his victory to the Peróns. He returned a hero, and Evita not only gave him a brand new house but got one of the town's best furniture dealers to furnish it in style. Then she persuaded the dealer to tear up the bill as a patriotic gesture.

Even the opposition newspapers could not avoid a good human interest story like that, although they inevitably embroidered it with sarcastic comment. But that did not matter. For within a year of her husband becoming president, Evita owned or controlled the four principal radio stations in Buenos Aires and, through her influence over the Ministry of Information, exercised virtual censorship rights over the news content on all of Argentina's 33 radio stations. She owned two large Buenos Aires daily newspapers — *Democracia* and *El Mundo* — bought through the generous help of business friends, and there were many other Perónista newspapers throughout the country which marched to the beat of her drum. But more important than that, she knew how to use radio and newspapers in a way they had never been used before anywhere in Latin America.

There was never a day when *Democracia* did not run at least five pictures of *La Señora Presidenta* in the paper, all of them taken by her own personal photographer who never left her side from early morning until she returned home at night. She also knew how to extract the last possible drop of propaganda value from situations that normally would be regarded as bureaucratically dry and colourless.

When the national census was taken in 1947, she and Perón devoted several days to popularising the work of the small army of census gatherers by going out themselves into the slums of the city. In each home they visited, the President would take down the statistical details while his wife distributed gifts among the women and children who swarmed around.

It was hardly any wonder that working people looked upon her as a beautiful goddess. Wherever she went in Argentina men knelt in the dust to spell out Evita in flowers for her to walk upon. She appeared before them at monster demonstrations, a young woman in her twenties, dressed in the latest Paris fashions, draped in mink and glittering in diamonds. 'You, too, will have clothes like these some day,' she promised them. From the balcony of the Casa Rosada, she harangued them with a torrent of words that made them ready to die for her. 'I speak in the name of the humble, the homeless, to cry out against the old evil days,' her voice would blast out across the packed plaza in front of the palace. Her political philosophy was simple: love for the poor, hatred of the rich. It was no matter that her enemies sneered at the demagoguery of it all. There were millions of Argentines who believed that she was passionately, sincerely determined to give them something they had never known before — respect, dignity, and a place in the Argentine sun.

It was a respect she demanded for herself, and those who failed to show it were ruthlessly pursued. The unbending bluebloods of the Sociedad de Beneficencia were soon to pay for their refusal to make her their president. Their charity was forced to close down when the Government cut off its annual subsidy, which was then turned over to Evita who had started her own welfare organisation with £500 of her own money. To those rich ladies who had little else to do other than devote their lives to 'good works', it was the most disgraceful thing that had ever happened, and worse, their husbands, whose words were once law in the land, had actually allowed that woman to get away with it. Their husbands could only shrug.

Power no longer went hand-in-hand with money in the new Argentina of the Peróns. Men accustomed through birth, education and family tradition to govern now humiliatingly watched their tongues in front of their maids and farm workers. Hostesses at dinner tables fixed frozen smiles on guests who criticised the Peróns in the presence of servants. The same discretion had to be observed in taxicabs, trolley cars, and offices. Everybody earning a wage in Argentina were Perónistas, it seemed. Cooks put up portraits of Evita and the General on the kitchen wall. Chambermaids listened to him on the radio. Gardeners, factory hands, and office workers joined in demonstrations for him and his wife. It was a time for discretion by people who thought otherwise.

For the first time since the days of the bloody tyrant Rosas, Argentines looked over their shoulders before expressing critical opinions. They had good reason to. The gaols were full of people who had failed to take precaution, even though Perón had publicly ordered a general amnesty for 14,000 political prisoners on the day of his inauguration. Only a few were actually released, however, and a month later he quietly rescinded the amnesty. But just in case there were still Argentines around who were blind or foolish enough to think that their friends were unduly paranoiac in their fear of eaves-droppers, one of Perón's closest confidants, Rear Admiral Alberto Teisaire, casually admitted one day that 'we know that many people express opinions against us even in cafés.' Asked how he knew this, the Admiral replied: 'We have people informing us.' Each week, newspapers in Buenos Aires published lists of the café arrests — those people who had talked too much in their cups. The *oyentes*, as the listeners were called, did not restrict themselves to bar-room chatter. They tuned in to telephone conversations as well, and the Government made no secret of that, either. After months of speculation about telephone-tapping, the Casa Rosada issued a statement admitting it with the justification that telephones 'may not be abandoned to the thoughtless or irresponsible. Employing the telephone to insult or offend is a crime which deserves punishment by justice. The long arm of the law and the Department of Posts and Telegraphs watch over the use of the telephone, that its noble and social purpose should not be misused. Such irresponsible criminals will be punished.'

In the general atmosphere of fear, Argentines were still able to joke about their situation — though they usually did so in the privacy of their homes and only among the closest of friends. One favourite story floating around the cocktail circuit poked fun at Perón's secret police, the pervasive army of men in gaberdine raincoats who were always conspicuous wherever Argentines gathered. Apparently a tramcar passenger foolishly gave vent to his feelings about a 'government of petty politicians, rogues and fools, incompetent, corrupt, and costly,' As he got off the tram, he was tapped on the shoulder. 'I must arrest you,' said one of his fellow tramcar passenger, producing a federal police badge from his raincoat pocket. 'It's not permitted to speak about our Government that way.' Thinking quickly, the other passenger angrily told him his hearing was defective, that he had been talking about the American Government. For a second policeman was silent. Then he smiled grimly: 'No,' he said, 'you are not getting away with that. There aren't two governments like the one you've described.' There was a similar story about the Chilean dog and the Argentine dog. The Chilean dog, underfed and disease-ridden, decided to go to Argentina where there was always plenty to eat. On the Andean mountain pass frontier between the two countries he met an Argentine dog, well-fed and healthy-looking, who was going the other way into Chile. That surprised the Chilean dog who wanted to know why he was going to Chile when the food was so good in Argentina. 'Simple,' said the Argentine dog. 'I want to bark.'

These stories were harmless enough. But there was one joker who managed to turn both Peróns apoplectic with rage. One morning a sign was found hanging from a lamp-post near their Alvear Avenue residence. Written on it were the words: 'This post is waiting for President Perón.' What made the message more chilling was its exquisite timing. It came right after a bloody revolution in Bolivia, which borders Argentina to the north. The President there, Gilberto Villarroel, who had gained power through an Argentine-engineered coup d'etat, was dragged from the presidential palace and hung from a lamp-post in the city's main plaza. It had been a damaging blow to Argentine pride, undercutting its influence in the hemisphere, and particularly annoying to Peron who had played a major role in putting his good friend Villarroel into Bolivia's presidential palace in the first place. But there was nothing he could do about it — his South American neighbours, not to mention the US — were watching Argentina too closely for that, though he might well have been tempted to follow the example of Queen Victoria, who, after being severely provoked by a Bolivian dictator who had manhandled her ambassador and finding there was nothing her mightly imperial empire could do about it, took a pen and crossed the mountainous country off her map.

But Perón certainly reacted to the hint that some Argentines wanted him to suffer the same fate as President Villarroel. From his presidential balcony he growled that if anyone in Argentina was thinking of starting a revolt he himself would 'act the week before,' and he warned that he had the 'necessary force' to do so. 'It is all a matter of giving a few feet of rope to my descamisados and then we will see who hangs.' To a roar of agreement from the throng massed in the plaza below, he claimed that he had 500,000 workers behind him and, 'as Napoleon said, with me at the head that amounts to one million.'

Such indulgent boasting was not Evita's style. With blunt directness she told her descamisados how to deal with enemies: 'Whoever speaks ill of the Government, give him what he deserves. Let's not try and convince him.' So when naval cadets coughed loudly during a newsreel of Evita, twenty of them were immediately expelled from the Naval College, and when an opposition Deputy introduced a bill in Congress to forbid public activity by officials' wives — an obvious attack on her — she had him stripped of his Congressional immunity and thrown in jail.

She embarked on a vendetta against *La Prensa*, the finest of Argentina's newspapers. With a circulation of 460,000 a day and 570,000 on Sundays, the paper under the editorship of its owner, Alberto Gainza Paz, the head of one of Argentina's leading families and an oligarch of the old school, spearheaded the opposition to the Perons. Defiantly, it editorialised 'we do not need mentors or tutors or prophets or redeemers or protectors or saviours.' As for *La Presidenta*, it refused to mention her by name, referring to her in news columns when it had to as 'the wife of the President,'

But as was so often the case in battles involving Evita, it was something much more personal that sparked her relentless, uncompromising war with a paper that over the years had earned an international reputation for excellence. And, as with the ladies of the Sociedad de Beneficienca, it was a social snub that aroused her fury. As the wife of the President she expected the city's major newspapers to automatically cover any social event, cocktail party or diplomatic dinner, she held in the Residence or the Casa Rosada. But even the most glittering of receptions went unmentioned in the society pages of *La Prensa*, an insult that placed Gainza Paz, as far as she was concerned, in the same category as the rest of the country's oligarchs who so bitterly despised her.

'I will make them pay for all the suffering they caused the poor — to the last drop of blood left in them,' she cried as she poured out the bitterness of her feelings from the balcony of the Casa Rosada. Sure enough, *La Prensa* soon began to pay for its opposition. In January of 1947, pro-Perón demonstrators attacked *La Prensa*'s gray building on Avenida de Mayo and started fires which were put out by the staff. For a while it looked as though the paper would suffer the same fate as *Critica*, which during the turbulent October days of 1945 had been attacked with machine guns and bombs and set on fire by Perónista mobs. The editor fled to Uruguay and the owner, a widow, had promptly sold out to Perón. But Gainza Paz was made of sterner stuff. He held on although the verbal attacks continued. Meanwhile, Evita had not yet finished with the ladies of the Sociedad de Beneficiencia. For suddenly a god-sent opportunity for revenge presented itself. The society's leader, its most aristocratic member, Dona Maria Unzue de Alvear, died at the age of 88. Among her good works she had built and endowed a church, and the family expected to bury her in its crypt. But Evita dug up an ancient sanitation ordinance which prevented the old lady from being buried anywhere except in a cemetery. The family ignored it. But when the cortege set out, it was stopped by the police and turned back. So, with the satisfaction of having pursued her vengeance to the grave, Evita set off on a trip to Europe. Soon she was to be as famous (or notorious) around the world as she was at home.

7

EUROPEAN ADVENTURE

Evita's enemies — she called them her super-critics — said she was a *resentida*, meaning she had a chip on her shoulder, that everything she did was motivated by jealousy and hatred for the class who had treated her like dirt as a child. She felt sufficiently sensitive about the charge to dispute it in her autobiography. 'I fight against all the privileges of power and wealth. That is to say, against all the oligarchy, not because the oligarchy has ill-treated me at any time. On the contrary. Until I arrived in the position I now occupy in the Perónista movement I owed them nothing but attentions, including one group representing the ladies of oligarchy who offered to introduce me to their highest circles. My special resentment does not come from hatred at all.' Understandably, those who remembered her bitter battles with the ladies of the Sociedad de Beneficiencia, could only smile. They believed she not only hated those women but was determined to make them aware every second of the day that she was going to be wealthier, more powerful than they ever had been or could ever hope to be. Evita's European Tour made that point.

The yearly trips to Europe formed part of the lifestyle of most well-bred Argentine families. Although Spain was the ancestral home of many of them, they usually left out Madrid and headed straight for Paris, where they soaked up the culture and spent lavishly on the latest fashions. Evita's chance to follow in their footsteps came in April 1947 when Spanish dictator Francisco Franco awarded her a high decoration. He announced that 'wishing to give a proof of my esteem to Dona Maria Eva Duarte de Perón, I hereby grant her the Grand Cross of the Order of Isabel the Catholic.' Some cynics promptly attributed General Franco's sudden show of affection for Senora Perón to his country's urgent need for Argentine wheat. True or not, he soon found out that both the gesture and the wheat were going to prove a little more expensive than he had anticipated. He received word from his ambassador in Argentina that the President's wife intended to pick up the honour herself.

Perón's Foreign Minister, Juan Atilio Bramuglia, had advised against the trip on the grounds that Argentina was currently trying to mend fences with the United States and a visit at that time by the wife of Argentina's President to fascist Spain would not be looked upon with favour in Washington. But Evita ignored the advice, and Bramuglia was later to pay dearly for having given it. The only other voice raised openly in protest was a mysterious phantom who somehow managed to cut into President Perón's ceremonial farewell broadcast which was being carried live on a nation-wide radio hook-up. Using a clandestine transmitter which zeroed in to the state radio frequency, the broadcaster interrupted Perón to denounce 'those who proclaim themselves supporters of a false justice' before signing off with the words, 'Death to Perón.'

But her descamisados made up for that indignity. One hundred and fifty thousand of them turned up at Moron Airport the next moring to bid her a noisy, emotional farewell. 'I go to the Old World with a message of peace and hope,' she told them tearfully. 'I go as a representative of the working people, of my beloved descamisados, with whom, in going, I leave my heart.' Then, with one final embrace for her husband, she climbed aboard a Dakota of Spanish Iberian Airways, luxuriously refitted for the journey with a special bedroom and dining room.

Like the oligarchs she used to watch those summers of her childhood getting off the train at the dusty Los Toldos railway station surrounded by a small army of family retainers, Evita took along maids, her hairdresser, dressmaker, doctor, secretaries, and her Jesuit confessor, Father Benitez. Her brother Juan went, too. She also took along 64 complete outfits, several fur coats, and a magnificent selection of jewellery.

For a girl who had never been further from Argentina than the occasional weekend trip across the river to the Uruguayan beach resort of Punte del Este with lovers during her early actress days, Evita was certainly travelling in style. An escort of 41 Spanish fighter planes accompanied the Dakota across the coast on the last stage of the journey into Madrid Airport. Guns boomed out a salute as the plane taxied along the runway to the red carpet where General Franco, his wife Carmen, and the entire Spanish Government stood waiting to greet their guest from Argentina.

There were another 200,000 ordinary Spaniards out there on the airport tarmac who had stood for hours in the blazing sun in the hope of catching a glimpse of the woman whose fame was already legendary. To poor Spaniards, who were among the poorest people in Europe, she was, as she was to poor Argentines, the *Dama de la Esperanza*, the Lady of Hope from the land of opportunity where so many of them still dreamed of living one day. They caught only a glimpse of her that evening at the airport — a flash of her blonde hair piled high in pompadour style and the shimmer and sparkle of her silk dress and jewels — before she was whisked off to General Franco's residence.

The next day, shops and offices were closed so that Madrilenians could gather in the plaza in front of the Palacio Real to listen to the loudspeakers broadcasting the ceremony in the Throne Room as Franco, in his uniform of Captain General of the Army and wearing the collar of the Order of San Martin that Peron had sent him, presented Evita with the highest decoration Spain can bestow, the diamond-encrusted Cross of Isabel the Catholic. Then, with the Generalissimo and his wife on either side, she moved out on to the balcony to greet the vast throng below. Her hosts were startled by the size and enthusiasm of the crowed. As Evita moved towards the microphones on the edge of the balcony, she turned to Franco with a smile: 'Any time you want to attract a crowd of this size, just give me a call.' Then she blew a kiss to the people below and spoke. 'I come as a rainbow between our two countries,' she told them. The crowd roared its appreciation and thousands of arms stretched out towards her in the falangist fascist salute. Evita, her shoulders draped in a mink coat despite the sweltering heat of a Madrid summer's day, responded by returning the salute. It was probably no more than a spontaneous gesture, done without thinking. But, as it turned out, that salute was to cost her nothing but trouble on the rest of her European tour.

Not in Franco's Spain, of course. There the people loved her.

At a folk dance in Madrid's Plaza Mayor which went on until three o'clock in the morning, each of the fifty provinces of Spain presented her with a complete outfit of a traditional costume. She was taken to see the bullfights in the Plaza de Toros where the arena was spread with coloured sand in the red and yellow national colours of Spain and the blue and white of Argentina, the coats of arms of the two countries etched out in the sand in the centre before disappearing under the lashing hooves of muira bulls especially selected for their ferociousness. There were gala banquets at Franco's palace of El Prado, and a tour of the provinces — Sevilla, Coruna, Galicia, Grenada, Catalonia. Wherever she went vast crowds of peasant women strained to touch the blonde goddess from Argentina. It was as though she was back home, bestowing her love, her dazzling smile, on her people, fondling babies, giving speeches and, most important of all, handing out her inexhaustible bounty — 100 peseta notes from a handbag that never emptied, and even Argentine land grants to would-be immigrants.

The *New York Times* special correspondent in Madrid reported that 'Senora Perón's wardrobe continues to be a rich source of conversation. In her many public appearance she has not worn the same outfit twice, and often she changes three or four times in a day. . . Some surprise was aroused by her appearance on the hottest day of the year so far in a magnificent mink cape, but there was also much admiration for her appearance. She dresses smartly, though with a certain tendency to overdress, and the women in Spain are taking a keen interest in observing what she wears. Beyond the superficial questions of what she looks like and how she dresses, her speeches have made a good impression. Whether she actually wrote her own speeches or not, they were cleverly written. They laid heavy emphasis on "social justice", a line that Franco has also been stressing more than usually of late. She speaks well, if somewhat theatrically — but that again is a style that goes over well with the Spaniards. There is a certain monotony in the constant stress on her love for the descamisados, but times are hard enough for most people in Spain so that they are interested in listening to anybody who wants to help the poor, and that is her constant theme.'

There was much talk among Spanish aristocrats about their unwillingness to meet Evita. However, they were never given an opportunity to live up to their talk as none of them were invited. In fact, when the wife of the ex-king of Rumania sent a message to Señora Perón that she would like to meet her, the response was brutal: 'Let her stand out in the street like everybody else.'

Even Franco felt the rough edge of her tongue on one occasion. When she told him that Argentina would be sending him two shiploads of wheat as a thank-you gift, the Generalissimo foolishly demurred. 'We don't need wheat,' he told her. 'We have so much flour we don't know what to do with it.' That was such a palpable lie that Evita looked at him quizzically for a second and then snapped: 'Why not try putting it in the bread?' If that retort disturbed Franco's dictatorial equilibrium, he quickly recovered. He had, after all, spent nearly a million dollars on his guest's visit. So he smiled that weary, tight-lipped smile of his and tried to ignore the fact that no one had talked like that to him for years.

As for Evita, her rainbow shimmered undimmed across Spain. At the end of her two weeks and four days, she spoke to the women of Spain in a nation-wide broadcast. 'I feel drunk with love and happiness,' she told them, 'because my simple woman's heart has begun to vibrate with the eternal chords of immortal Spain.' With that, she flew off to Rome.

Perhaps it was the era — the shabby, depressing period of post-war austerity and poverty — that made Evita's progress across Europe so fascinating. Popular tabloid newspapers followed her every move in breathless detail while even such heavyweights as *The Times* pondered over the significance of it all. *Time* magazine even put Evita on its cover, an honour not particularly appreciated by the Argentine Government which banned the magazine probably because of one or two snide phrases. But the cover story started off in mild enough manner with a carpenter in faded blue denim hammering together a temporary grandstand on Avenida Alvear. He was not sure what it was for. 'Perhaps for the return of the Señora from her voyage. Ah, Señor, you have read of this voyage. A miracle, is it not so? Surely, all the world must know about it.'

Meanwhile, there was Italy. The Italians had arranged the most lavish reception their country had accorded anyone since the war. Of course there was a close bond between the two countries. Over the years, Italy had sent many hundreds of thousands of unemployed, impoverished peasants across the sea to start new lives in Argentina, and probably a majority of

Argentine families looked upon Italy as their ancestral home. In fact, the Italian Government was hoping that its welcome for its illustrious guest, while not on the opulent scale of General Franco's, would help pave the way for a new wave of emigrants to lighten the burden of post-war recovery. So, as Evita's plane crossed over the Italian island of Sardinia, two bombers of the Italian Air Force joined it to act as escorts for the final 200 miles to the mainland.

As Evita stepped from the plane, Italy's 75-year-old Foreign Minister, Count Carlo Sforza, bent low over her hand. Two thousand children waved paper Argentine and Italian flags. A band played, drowning out the wolf-whistles of American airmen gazing admiringly at the blonde in the flower-printed skin-tight dress. At the airport gate, eight elaborately uniformed carabinieri on white horses saluted with swords as Evita set off in a 50-car procession down the Appian Way into Rome. Posters on house walls hailed her as the 'gentle ambassadress' of a nation which chose during the 'recent painful war' not to join in the 'bloc of powers which stood against Italy.'

The cavalcade passed the Trevi and Essedra fountains, dry since the war but splashing again for the duration of the distinguished visitor's stay. The street for the last mile to the Argentine Embassy, where Evita was staying, had been repaved and, as part of a hurried beautification project, a landmark pavement urinal in front of the embassy had been removed.

Inside the embassy, almost £75,000 had been spent in a frenzied rush to smarten up. The driveway had been repaved in polished green marble (no car had been allowed on it before she arrived). The courtyard was rebuilt as a sunken garden with fountain, flagged walks and flower-beds. Two new marble staircases were constructed inside. The furniture was re-upholstered and the walls repainted, and pictures of President Perón hung in every room, including the bathrooms, of the five-storey building. There were two in Eva's bedroom — an oil painting over the bed and a small photo in a gaudy gilt frame on her dresser. The room had been refurbished in her favourite Louis XV style. But, sadly for all the money spent, the impression was ruined within seconds of Evita's arrival.

Several thousand Italians had gathered outside the embassy, and cries of 'Perón, Perón' brought Evita out on to her balcony. She waved, and arms in the crowd responded with the straight-armed fascist salute which had not been seen in Italy since the overthrow of the Mussolini dictatorship. Immediately, fierce fighting broke out as the fascists were charged by screaming communists. A horrified Evita fled back into her room, covering her ears to drown out the boos and catcalls of the mob outside. It took Italian riot police an hour to clear the street, by which time the beautiful flower-beds outside the embassy had been trampled out of existence.

The chief of protocol in the Foreign Ministry hurried around early the next morning to offer his apologies. But it was a pale and strained-looking young woman who drove with a strong police escort to the Vatican to see Pope Pius XII. She was dressed in a long-sleeved dress of heavy black silk, reaching from her throat to the floor. Her elaborate coils of blonde hair were covered with a delicate black lace mantilla. She wore lace gloves and just one piece of jewellery — the blue and silver star of Isabel which Franco had given her. She was a bewitchingly beautiful sight as she walked past the Swiss Guards on the arm of the one-eyed Prince Allessandro Ruspoli who was dressed in elegant court knee breeches.

For Evita, this was the big moment of her Italian visit. She had told friends that she expected to receive a papal marquisate for her work with the poor of Argentina. It would certainly have elevated her to the very highest social standing in Argentina. The good ladies of the Sociedad de Beneficiencia would have found it embarrassingly difficult to ignore her after that. But it was not to be.

The Pope received her in his study with all the pomp that Vatican ceremonial prescribes for the wives of heads of state. He thanked her for her work among the poor and he told her that he was presenting her husband with the Cross of the Order of Pope Pius IX, a magnificent eight-pointed star laden with diamonds but not quite the highest decoration in the papal hierarchy. At the end of the audience, the Pope gave Evita a rosary, the usual gift on such occasions.

But there were compensations — luncheon with the Foreign Minister, a Grand Hotel reception glittering with papal titles, and a dazzling performance of *Aida* under the stars in the ancient Baths of Caracalla. Eva, in black flowered silk with a white fox cape, her hair, ear lobes, and shapely neck glittering with diamonds, arrived on the arm of Prime Minister de Gasperi, just in time to delay the second act a full half hour. Some of the paying guests were furious. But the Latin American diplomats who had been given the best seats, gave her a rousing welcome. It must have been quite a moment for Evita Perón. She had come a long way from that one room shack in Los Toldos. But no matter how high she stood, the sneers, the put-downs always pursued her.

Time magazine, in a style so uniquely its own in those days, quoted an interview that Evita had apparently given to a reporter (though it neither mentioned the name of the reporter nor the location of the interview, giving rise to suspicions that the story was the product of *Time's* fertile imagination). '''I like all music, concerts, and operas — especially Chopin,'' said Eva . . . admitting that her Italian reception, despite the communists, had been ''enchanting''. ''I don't understand politics,'' she continued, her alabaster hands fluttering expressively, but ''I am profoundly religious.'' The Pope had been ''marvellous''. ''What saintliness,'' said Eva Perón, her brown eyes rolling heavenward. The reporter asked if she enjoyed reading as much as music. ''Oh yes,'' said Eva. And did she have any favourites? ''Why do people ask me questions like that? I like everything I read.'' But surely she must have some favourites. ''Well,'' said Eva, her brow furrowed in agonized thought, ''Plutarch,'' ''He's an ancient writer'', she added hastily.'' *Time* got itself banned in Argentina for a while for that little bit of maliciousness.

Evita's first public remarks in Rome, to an audience of 600 women, sounded more like her. 'I have a name that has become a battle-cry throughout the world,' she told them. 'In this first speech I make in this immortal city, I want to say that women have the same duties as men and therefore should have the same rights . . . In Argentina, social justice is evidently a fact and the purpose of General Perón's programme is to bring about a moral and material evolution of the masses, especially women. Viva Italia.' The women loved her, swept up by her fierce, passionate rhetoric.

It was a different story in the industrial cities of the north, strongholds of the country's communists and socialists. She was booed and hissed in Milan and visibly frightened by screaming mobs that tried to attack her limousine (one of the million spiteful stories about Evita had her angrily turning to her escort, a retired senior naval officer, and complaining: 'Did you hear they called me a whore?' 'Think nothing of it, Senora,' said the officer soothingly. 'I haven't been to sea for 15 years, and they still call me admiral.') Her next stop was supposed to be Venice, where gondoliers were to serenade her in a lantern-lit evening parade through the canals. But when she heard that Premier de Gasperi had been shouted down by a left-wing mob the day before in Venice, Evita abandoned the north and hurried back to Rome.

An embarrassed Italian government official attributed the change in their guest's plans to the heat (Europe sweltered in a scorching heat-wave that summer) and to a stiff schedule which had finally become too exhausting. But he admitted there could have been 'other considerations'. A spokesman for the Government's ruling Christian Democratic Party indignantly supplied those: 'It was,' he said, the first time in our 2,000-year history that a woman guest had been insulted in our country. Fortunately, he was talking about a woman who had been toughened to a lifetime of insults. After a few days relaxing on the shores of Lake Como, she bounced back, ready for the next stage of her European odyssey — Paris the home of wealthy Argentines, the Mecca of their oligarch culture.

The weather was still cruel. At Orly Airfield the temperature stood at 90 degrees when Evita stepped down from her Dakota to be greeted by Foreign Minister Georges Bidault bending low to kiss her hand. She had kept her finest clothes for Paris and looked a dazzling sight, white suit, white shoes, white handbag, and a big white straw hat. A large ruby clip was her only jewel, apart from the three rings she always wore on the fourth finger of her left hand — a broad gold wedding ring, an enormous solitaire diamond (reputed to be second only in size to that of the wife of the Aga Khan), and a sapphire, ruby, and emerald eternity ring.

'This is a massacre,' she laughed as Bidault led her through a throng of pushing, struggling cameramen and a cheering contingent of Argentine diplomats to the motorcade that whisked her off to the Ritz. Outside the hotel, eighteen French war orphans piped 'Vive l'Argentine'. She hugged and kissed two of them, leaving smears of scarlet lipstick on their cheeks.

In succeeding days there was a luncheon with President Vincent Auriol at the Chateau de Rambouillet, where she appeared in a glamorous draped dress of white printed with large blue-green flowers, then dinner with Foreign Minister Bidault, a visit to Versailles, and a reception at the Cercle d'Amerique-Latine in the Avenue d'Iena, where the whole Latin American diplomatic corps filed before her — the women curtseying and walking backward three paces. She wore for this occasion the most sumptuous costume of them all — an off-the-shoulder, cloth-of-gold evening gown which clung to her body like a mermaid's skin. With it she wore an enormous jewelled necklace, long earings to match, three jewelled bracelets, and a gold lamé veil falling from her blonde pompadour hair to the end of the fish-train on her gown. High-heeled golden sandals with stone-studded heels flashed and caught everybody's eye as she took the marble staircase, clasping her train. In the early hours of the following morning she supped in the fashionable Pre-Catelan restaurant in the Bois de Boulogne, where her fellow diners stood on the tables under the trees to catch a glimpse of the visiting Presidenta.

A reporter for *Newsweek* magazine's Paris bureau, assigned to get a 'woman's eye view,' described Evita thus: 'She is 5 feet 5 but appears taller, with dark brown eyes (which are described as black), honey coloured hair with reddish glints (she can sit on her hair), and a very white skin which she accentuates by a pale foundation lotion, no rouge, and very dark lipstick. She has perfect teeth and her lips are parted in a permanent, if wearying, smile. This is because she speaks neither French nor English and must contrive to appear interested. She neither smokes nor drinks and has a tendency to put on weight alarmingly, so she has a daily massage and a daily checkup by her doctor. She eats sparingly, and a member of her suite disappears into the kitchens, wherever she happens to be eating. She found that summer in Paris was hotter than in Argentina, and made a remark several times in the Cercle d'Amerique-Latine to the effect that it is always cooler if the doors remain closed and the hot air is kept out.'

She was wilting visibly as the temperatures stayed up in the high nineties day after day. People close to her said she was very tired and had been sleeping badly. Used to a straight-forward diet of *bife* and *papas fritas* (steak and chips), she found the rich French food and champagne intolerably indigestible as she did the tasteless cornbread she was served at every meal, which was no doubt a polite way of emphasising French need for Argentine wheat. So rich was Argentina, so poor the great old nations of Europe, that Evita could play the benefactress wherever she went — Spain, Italy, even France — with pesetas, pesos, francs from her handbag for the poor and giant loans for their governments. Indeed, one of the high points of her stay in Paris came at the Quai d'Orsay, where she presided in grande dame manner over the signing of a French-Argentine commercial treaty granting France a loan of 600 million pesos (about 120 million dollars). It would buy a lot of Argentine wheat, and beef

90

as well, although that didn't prevent a less than gallant French newspaper from commenting rather churlishly that 'Madame Perón will be made palatable to the French workers and peasants by being dressed as a piece of Argentine frozen beef.'

Understandably, remarks like that dimmed Evita's enthusiasm for France. Her savoir faire began to slip a little. After asking four leading couturiers to give her an unprecedented private showing of their collections at the Ritz, Evita appeared an hour late, kept the models waiting in tiny dressing rooms with the temperature nearly a hundred degrees, then told them she did not have time to look at the gowns. Then there was another embarrassment at the super-elegant Restaurant des Ambassadeurs, where a pair of clowns dressed as a camel offered her a bouquet of flowers — through the rear-end of the camel. She was not amused and stalked out with her party to the sniggers of the other diners.

About one o'clock that morning, Evita phoned Buenos Aires and spoke to her husband. It had become a nightly routine for her to share the joys and griefs of the day with him. Evita sent off a package every night to Buenos Aires of all the pictures taken of her that day, and, wherever she stayed, her hosts always made sure there were photos of the General prominently displayed. They had never been apart so long, and they both must have felt the loneliness that goes hand-in-hand with power, surrounded by aides prepared to do their instant bidding, yet isolated, rather in the way of that old Irving Berlin melody — 'What'll I do with just a photograph to tell my troubles to?' The kind of troubles that neither aides nor photographs could solve, and which they most certainly must have discussed during those long nightly phone calls, included the question of whether she should or should not go to Great Britain.

The British Prime Minister Clement Attlee had invited her to his country after word had reached the Foreign Office via the British Embassy in Buenos Aires that an invitation would be appreciated. At first the British were delighted to get what they saw as an opportunity to put their rather strained relations with Argentina on a warmer footing. Perón had swept them economically from a country that they had long regarded as a sixth dominion. Their investments in Argentina had been reduced practically overnight from 250 million pounds to four million as a result of sales forced on them under the threat of expropriation. So they no longer possessed the kind of economic power over Argentina that fourteen years earlier had forced it to sign a trade pact that had included an agreement eliminating privately-owned Argentine bus lines in Buenos Aires for no other reason than that they threatened the profitability of the British-owned transport system in the city. But now all the British were concerned about was to safeguard their supplies of desperately needed beef. If that meant giving the wife of the Argentine President a few pleasant days in England then the British Government was happy to extend a warm welcome. Unfortunately, it did not work out in quite that way.

Basically the problem was that the British were finding it much more difficult to divest themselves of their colonial mentality than they were their empire, and Attlee's Labour Government handled the arrangements for the visit with all the tact and sensitivity of a nineteenth-century Tory gun-boat diplomatist. Responsibility for putting together a schedule was handed over to the Anglo-Hispanic Council whose secretary, it was announced, was well fitted to handle the matter because 'he has a close knowledge of Latin America. He was a Methodist missionary there, and has explored up the Amazon.' If that was not bad enough, the next word out of the Foreign Office was that arrangements were in hand 'to show Señora Perón things in which she is interested, such as the Royal Agricultural Show and the London Docks.' As an added attraction, Mrs Attlee had kindly offered to have tea with her.

If the Government thought it had everything under control, it was in for a big shock. That was not what the Señora wanted at all. First and foremost, she wanted to stay at Buckingham Palace with the King and Queen. That was all that mattered as far as she was concerned. It was to be the pinnacle, the supreme moment of her European Tour. Never again would her neighbours, those society ladies on Avenida Alvear, be able to look down on her.

So, suddenly, British Foreign Minister Ernest Bevin, whose beginnings in life were almost as humble as Evita's found himself with a diplomatic crisis on his hands. For not even a solid working-class socialist like Ernie Bevin could allow a woman with Evita's shady reputation to stay even one night under the roof of his Sovereign's palace. Word was passed to Evita that, unfortunately Their Majesties would not be in town during her visit. When her displeasure at that turn of events was leaked to the British press, a Foreign Office spokesman loftily commented on suggestions that there was some occasion for surprise that

Señora Perón would not be staying at Buckingham Palace. 'It is not a State visit,' he said. 'Such visits are extremely rare and to draw a comparison between them and a private visit is only proof of ignorance.'

Hastily, the Foreign Office made it clear that its spokesman was not referring to Señora Perón's ignorance. It was the newspapers, the ministry suggested, who had got it all wrong. The primary target of the FO's wrath was the tabloid *Sunday Pictorial* which had carried a front page streamer headline that 'The President's wife is not welcome'. The article said that the planned visit was 'causing increased embarrassment' to the Government. British members of Parliament were concerned because Señora Perón is 'the wife of a fascist dictator', because Argentina has 'consistently demanded pistol-point prices for meat that often proved to be of appalling quality', because she would come to Britain fresh from a 'triumphant reception in Franco's Spain, a country of oppression', and because 'the Señora's favourite party trick is to produce the fascist salute on the slightest pretext'.

That story was immediately picked up by the Associated Press wire service and transmitted to Argentina where it was gleefully carried by anti-Perónist newspapers. General Perón read it the next morning, and the AP promptly felt his wrath. The Ministry of Information put out a radio bulletin on the State network accusing the American wire service of being 'an instrument of certain interests engaged in disturbing good relations between Argentina and friendly countries'. Just who those certain interests were the Argentines did not say. But that same day, the British Ambassador was called to the Foreign Ministry in Buenos Aires and told that Señora Perón would not now be visiting Britain after all. There was no explanation. In London, British Ministers quietly heaved a sigh of relief, although naturally their Foreign Office spokesman voiced 'the liveliest regrets'.

So instead of Buckingham Palace, Evita had to make do with Switzerland, and just to add to her tale of woe, the Swiss gave her the most unpleasant reception of her whole trip. When the President drove with her from Berne station to the Town Hall, a young man who had pushed his way to the front of the curious crowd hurled two stones at the car, smashing the windscreen. Evita threw her hands up to protect her face. She was unhurt, and the stone-thrower was arrested after a struggle. The Swiss Government offered profuse apologies. But the next day, a group of young communists hurled tomatoes. They missed their target, striking the Foreign Minister who was sitting next to her and splattering her dress.

After two months on the road, Evita had finally had enough of Europe. She cut short her Swiss stay, flew to Dakar in West Africa, and there boarded an Argentine freighter, the *SS Buenos Aires*.

After voyaging across the Atlantic, she still had one final stop to make, disembarking in Rio de Janeiro just in time to upstage the continent's first post-war Inter-American Defence Conference. The night before she arrived, the Argentine Embassy papered the city with thousands of huge ochre-tinted posters of Evita. But by dawn the Brazilian police had taken them all down, and the Argentines were gently chided by the evening newspaper, *Diario da Noite*, with the comment that 'Brazilians don't need advice on how to treat beautiful charmers'. The Brazilian Foreign Minister decorated her with the Orden Nacional do Cruziero do Sul and then drove her the 40 miles to the fog-bound mountain valley where the conference was being held in the Quitandinha Hotel.

Now that she was back on Latin American soil that old magnetism of hers was beginning to work again. Special squads of police had to be rushed in from Rio to cope with the thousands of local people who swarmed into the hotel, eager to catch a glimpse of the Argentine goddess they had heard so much about. Escorted by the Foreign Ministers of both Brazil and Argentina, Evita made a dramatic entrance into the Quitandinha's salmon-pink conference salon just five minutes before US Secretary of State George Marshall began his keynote speech. Delegates from every country in the hemisphere rose to applaud her as she took her seat in a specially roped-off section in the front of the hall by the speaker's rostrum.

Later she drank champagne with Marshall who told her that her country's representative at the conference, Foreign Minister Juan Bramuglia, had become everybody's hero. From his hotel room, sipping maté from a silver gourd, Bramuglia had set aside years of Argentine animosity and distrust of American intentions in the continent, managing to orchestrate the necessary compromises whenever delegates appeared bogged down in disputes as they worked their way towards a treaty that would bind all the nations in the Americas to mutual defence. Evita smiled a watery smile at this fulsome praise for Juan Bramuglia. Indeed, Secretary Marshall unknowingly could not have done his Argentine colleague a greater disservice. As Evita set off on her last lap home, she gave much thought to her husband's foreign minister and the reputation he was making for himself.

8

'LOVE CONQUERS ALL'

Undoubtedly the noisiest place in the world on August 23, 1947, was the port of Buenos Aires. Evita was coming home. A chill breeze off the Rio de la Plata whipped the muddy water-front as her ship slipped past the old yacht club of the oligarchs and pulled into harbour. Sirens howled. Tugs boomed their welcome. On the dockside, 250,000 Argentines roared a greeting: *'Uno, dos, tres, Evita otra vez!'* (One, two, three, Evita once again!). Thousands of them had poured into the capital by train and bus the previous day, sleeping out in the city parks, wrapped in their ponchos to protect them from the cold winter night air. Their dark skins, Indian-mestizo features, and ragged clothes — the badge of the descamisados, Evita's Shirtless Ones — were their passport to the dockside festivities.

Amid the din, the ship inched up against the quay. Evita was on the bridge, waving and wiping the tears from her eyes. Her husband-president was crying, too. For in Latin America, a man is allowed to show his emotion. He is not considered any less of a man for that. As his wife stepped ashore, dressed in a kohinoor mink coat with luxurious balloon sleeves, he crushed her in an emotional embrace in front of the crowd. Then, with a flourish, Juan Domingo Perón wiped the tears from her eyes and led her to a specially-built platform draped with wine-coloured velvet.

Obviously, it was a happy and exciting moment for both of

97

them. While the Grand Tour had had its ups and downs — diamonds in Madrid, boos in Milan — Eva Perón had become a world-famous figure. The Presidents of Spain and France had kissed her hand. She had met the Pope. She had stolen the limelight from US Secretary of State George Marshall. For two months her name had been in the headlines every day throughout Western Europe as newsmen scrambled over each other to cover every word and move of the illegitimate farm girl from the pampas. Every newspaper told and retold the astonishing rags to riches success story of the beautiful enchantress from Argentina.

It would not have been surprising if the Peróns had used those moments in front of the microphones for a little reflective glory and mutual back-slapping. Perhaps it says a lot about their characters, their single-minded devotion to power, that they used their few minutes with their descamisados and their captive nation-wide audience to attack their enemies. For even after nearly two years of close to dictatorial Perónista power, there were still opposition newspapers that refused to be silenced and political opponents who refused to be cowed. The President warned them on that August afternoon that his patience was exhausted and that if they did not accept his bid for tranquillity, it would be forced upon them.

'We have been tolerating the intolerable for the past year and a half,' he thundered. 'We are still asking that they do not use infamy as a battle nor calumny as a weapon. It is to their advantage that they listen to us: we want peace, we want tranquillity, because if some day they convince us that in order to obtain that tranquillity it is necessary to fight, we will fight! If tomorrow the moment should come to impose that peace by force I am decided to do so and on their shoulders will rest the responsibility.'

The crowds loved it. That was the kind of oligarch-bashing they had come to hear. They cheered even louder when their beloved Evita stepped forward to the microphones. First, she said softly, 'It is with profound emotion that I return to this my country where I left my three great loves, my homeland, my descamisados, and my beloved General Perón.' Then she, too, turned on her enemies. She had heard disturbing rumours in Europe and Rio, she cried, 'But whatever the future promises, if I fall, I will fall with my beloved descamisados, and at the side of General Perón.'

And yet whatever it was she had heard, this hardly seemed the right moment for such sabre-rattling. For barring a few boos in middle-class suburban cinemas when pictures of her return were shown on the newsreel programmes that precede every film in Argentina, she had received the most tumultuous welcome ever staged for any woman in the Americas. While church bells rang out throughout the nation, a thanksgiving mass was held in the main cathedral in Buenos Aires. Airplanes dropped olive twigs, tied with the ribbons of flags of all nations, over the city. Coloured pigeons — dyed pink and blue (a task that occupied the attention of lowly Perónista functionaries for days) — fluttered across the central plazas of the capital. It was an outpouring of love, genuine as well as organised, on a scale that even that admittedly emotional nation had never known before. A writer for the *New Yorker* magazine caught the mood of the moment with an article called 'Love, Love, Love'. 'The classic pulp romance of our time,' wrote Philip Hamburger, may well turn out to be 'The fabulous Adventures of Juan and Eva Perón, or Love Conquers All.'

Hamburger wrote that on his first day in Buenos Aires, he was lunching in a restaurant on one of the main downtown streets, sampling a practically raw sirloin the size of a telephone directory, when he heard a shrill honking of horns. He looked out of the window and saw a long parade of trucks that had halted, snarling traffic. 'The drivers were just sitting in their cabs, grinning and blowing their horns. On the side of each truck were crude posters bearing pictures of red hearts pierced by arrows, and mingled with the hearts, inscriptions reading: 'Eva, We Love You,' 'Eva and Juan, a Blessed Couple,' 'You Will Go to Heaven, Eva and Juan,' and so on.' Thinking that it was a satiric attack on the administration and perhaps the beginning of a revolution, he paid his bill and went out into the street to get a closer look.

'Hundreds of people, mostly pale, thin little men with tiny black moustaches, were glancing at the posters as they rushed past, presumably on their way to a steak lunch. Hundreds of other people were peering from the windows of the tall, modern buildings along the street. The unceasing sound of the horns, the truck drivers' foolish grins, and the mocking, insolent signs shimmering in the bright sunlight gave the scene a momentous and historic air.'

'This is it,' he thought. 'The Perón police will come. They will destroy these seditious posters. Heads will roll.' He stood there for quite a while. The police did not come. The only policeman

99

he saw was standing on a white wooden platform in the middle of the cross-roads, and he was simply shrieking at the driver of a huge bus, who, delayed by the cavalcade of trucks, had begun to honk his horn.

Finally, he caught sight of a North American friend of his, a long-time resident in Argentina, in the crowd. He grasped his arm. 'Revolution?' he asked, pointing at one of the signs. 'Revolution, hell,' his friend said. 'Just a demonstration of affection. The trucking union is about to strike. They want to make certain in advance that Juan and Eva are on their side.' The friend looked again at the signs. 'Very good,' he said. 'Properly affectionate. They'll probably win the strike.'

In Argentina, Hamburger wrote, 'love makes the Peróns go round. Their whole act is based on it. They are constantly, madly, passionately, nationally in love. They conduct their affair with the people quite openly. They are the perfect lovers — generous, kind, and forever thoughtful, in matters both large and small. Their love is all-encompassing, ever present. It settles like a soft blanket over the loved ones, providing warmth and protection and the opportunity for a good, long sleep.'

But there were still plenty of Argentines who did not love the Peróns. Not that there was anything they could do about it except exchange gossip and rumours — there were plenty of these, told at fashionable cocktail parties and dinners. At one dinner party a guest had learned that the Señor and Señora were splitting up. Just that morning, he had heard from a man who knew a man who had a friend who worked in the President's office, in the Casa Rosada, that the Señora often screamed at the President and that her voice could be heard down the corridor outside his chambers. This split, the guest continued, was quite in line with the rumour that the Señora coveted the Presidency herself and had secretly ordered the printing of hundreds of thousands of posters bearing her picture and the words 'The First Woman President'. 'When the time comes,' the guest said, 'she will poison him.' Another guest was also flushed with rumour. The President, he said, was fascinated by the Señora. In her presence, he acted like a lovesick adolescent. At official dinner parties, she would endlessly relate details of her famous trip abroad, and the President would clap his hands at each tiresome incident and cry, 'Wonderful, wonderful!' But the party's hostess said she had been told that the President was tired of the Señora and was considering forcing her into exile. When she insisted on boring dinner guests with reminiscences about her trip, he would ostentatiously drop his chin onto his chest and make rude snoring sounds.

Certain stories were staples. When the Señora autographed pictures, she always misspelled most of the words of her inscription; the Señora had left huge unpaid bills behind her in Rome; every evening after work she repaired to the Central Bank, where she drank 'real French champagne' with the directors and plotted the undermining of the nation's financial structure; she carried about with her several million pesos in cash, in a little black bag; she had recently bought a £550,000 diamond from Cartier's in Paris; at dinner parties she admired the jewellery of other female guests with such feline emphasis that she was invariably presented with it before the end of the evening.

However, the telling and retelling of such gossip did little to lift the heavy air of depression and dejection that pervaded the city. The country's intellectuals — students, writers, artists — were depressed by a sense of inevitability, frustration, and gathering darkness. A middle-aged lawyer recalled his student days in the 1940s. 'On this continent,' he said, 'we were accustomed to the dictator type of rulers — ruthless, arrogant strongmen. It is a woeful tradition. But this man Perón, he was a dictator of another type. He was subtle, devious, charming. He did not come out in the open and crack skulls. He did his work silently and cynically. You see, there was so little we could put our hands on — everything he did was in the name of demo-cracy and social betterment — and yet we sensed the smell of evil in the air, and the thin ledge on which we walked.'

9

EVA'S RULE

In the early hours of September 24, 1948, Buenos Aires radio stations began blaring forth the news of a conspiracy to murder Evita and her husband. Thirteen of the plotters had already been arrested said Federal Police Chief Arturo Bertollo in a dawn press conference. He named their leader, and it was hard to believe. For it was the original descamisado, Cipriano Reyes, leader of the meat packing house workers. Three years earlier, on that fateful October 17, he had led his ragged mob of fellow workers into the heart of Buenos Aires and had restored Juan Perón to power. Now, if it was true, Reyes, disillusioned and in opposition, had planned to throw a bomb at the Peróns as they entered the Teatro Colon Opera House for a gala performance. Also accused as a plotter was a former American Embassy official, John D. Griffiths, who had been ordered out of the country the previous April for alleged anti-Perón activities. No explanation for this desperate adventure was given by the police. But within a few hours posters denouncing the plot were plastered around the city. Loudspeaker trucks toured the streets announcing a one-day general strike so that workers could show their indignation. By noon the city was paralysed.

Factories and shops closed. The trains stopped running. So to make sure of a good turnout, the government mobilised trucks to bring in workers from the outlying shanty-town slums to the centre of the city. In the bright spring sunlight they streamed into Plaza de Mayo, many of them carrying posters condemning the plot against their beloved leaders. Gallows decorated trees and buildings — a meaningful reminder of the bitter speech two weeks earlier in which Perón assured his enemies that his voice would not tremble as he ordered them hanged. 'To the gallows with Cipriano,' screamed the vast crowd in the plaza. But then, as the afternoon grew later, the chanting changed to the more familiar rhythmic 'Evita! Evita! Perón! Perón!' There was a roar that lasted for a good ten to fifteen minutes when finally the President and this wife walked out on to the balcony, accompanied by Interior Minister Angel C. Borlenghi.

When the crowd had quietened down sufficiently for Peron to begin to speak, he launched into an emotional, almost hysterical attack on 'the traitors to the country' who had plotted his death because 'international capitalists desire it.' His audience knew the Peron shorthand by heart. 'It's the Yankees,' they yelled. The President was not saying anything. But he savagely attacked John Griffiths as 'this international spy who came into our country free and trusted, only to use his diplomatic position to spy against the Republic.' Then Evita weighed in with a promise that she would willingly 'die a thousand times' for her descamisados, and she wondered aloud, with a catch in her voice, why anybody would want to kill a 'humble woman' just because she happened to be the 'humblest collaborator of General Perón'. Below in the plaza, the crowd responded with a thunderous 'Hang them, hang them!'

But before things got out of hand, Perón called on everybody to be calm. He had the patience, he said, 'to dominate the agitators or liquidate them if necessary.' He told them to go home, adding an afterthought with a grin that they should not stop and attack *La Prensa* on their way, which they had a habit of doing whenever they came into town for a Plaza de Mayo rally. Just what this one had been all about no one seemed quite sure. Not many Argentines, other than the most fanatical of Perónistas, took the story of the plot seriously.

John Griffiths, the American diplomat involved who was living on the other side of the River Plata in the Uruguayan capital of Montevideo, called it 'a joke in bad taste'. Cipriano Reyes was not heard from. Nor was he for another seven years. He was kept in gaol and intermittently tortured. Among the other alleged plotters were three priests, a half blind doctor, and two women, all of them completely unknown politically. As for

Glittering with diamonds in Paris on the arm of the Argentine Ambassador.

Touching up in Geneva.

Below: With her escorts at the Vatican, en route to see the Pope.

Back home, distributing gifts to children.

Preparing for a busy day with hairdresser and manicurist.

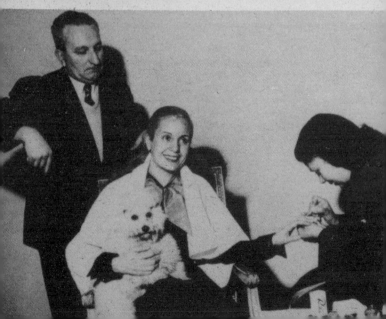

Above: The start of a formal evening.

Below: A gala night at the Teatro Colon opera house.

Above: A dying Evita greets the crowds from the balcony as she is held up by her husband, October 17, 1951.

Below: A warm embrace on that same "Santa Evita Day".

relations with the US, Perón seemed to have consigned them once more to the low level they had reached during his early days in power. There appeared to be only one reasonable explanation, that the Peróns wanted to warn their enemies, whoever they might be, they could still produce a potent mob of the faithful on short notice.

So it was attack, and there was no finer, fiercer exponent of that than Eva Perón. 'Wait until we get the opposition out of the way,' she told a group of union leaders who visited her in her office shortly after she returned from Europe. 'Then you'll really see things.' To a newly-elected Perónista deputy named Astorgano, a former bouncer in a bar who confessed he was nervous about speaking in Congress, she advised: 'Oh, you won't need to do much talking. But you can do plenty of listening. And if you hear anyone speaking ill of me, break his head open.'

One Congressional head that Evita particularly wanted bloodying belonged to Radical Deputy Ernesto Enrique Sammartino who had sardonically remarked on the floor of Congress that, 'A President who believes that the nation's history begins and ends with him shows at least a lack of mental and moral equilibrium.'

Perón paid no attention, preferring to joke about attacks like that unless they got out of hand. But not Evita. She was not going to allow an insult like that pass without punishment. She told Hector Campora, the president of the Chamber of Deputies, to expel Sammartino from Congress. Campora was a small-town dentist who had risen to the top in Perónista politics through a policy of slavish devotion to Evita which had paid off. He had once even boasted that, 'They say I'm Evita's servant. I'm honoured to be called her servant because I serve her loyally.' So naturally he wasted no time in carrying out her order.

Under Argentina's constitution, members of Congress could be expelled by a two-thirds vote for 'gross misconduct'. As far as Evita was concerned, there could be no greater misconduct than insulting her husband's dignity. There never was any doubt what the result would be. The Perónistas already controlled more than two-thirds of the Chamber of Deputies and they had one hundred per cent of the Senate. All the Radicals could do to protect their man was to stand up for him in debate. When Perónista Deputy Conte Grand put the expulsion motion before

105

the chamber, quoting Sammartino's attack on the President as the basis for the charge, a Radical deputy shouted, 'And well spoken, too!'

When it became time for Sammartino to defend himself, he spoke with measured insolence. 'We have not come here to do obeisance to the lash nor to dance to Madame Pompadour's tune,' he said. 'This is not a fashionable nightclub or the ante-room of a palace. It is the parliament of a free people, and it should be made plain to the people here and now that this Chamber will not obey the commands of meddling old colonels, nor heed orders given in perfumed letters from the boudoir of any ruler.' With that, Campora struck the bell on his desk and put an end to any further debate. A prominent Perónista hurried to a cloakroom telephone, then returned to whisper in Campora's ear. The roll call began, and the deputies voted — by turning the electrical indicators on their desk to 'Aye' or 'No'. The lights on the board above the dias flashed the result: 104 to 42 in favour of expulsion. 'Let's see who runs to telephone la Señora!' yelled Radical Deputy Emir Mercador.

With his parliamentary immunity lifted, Sammartino disappeared underground as federal police scoured the city for him. Finally, like so many other opponents of the Peróns, he surfaced across the river in Montevideo, from where he sent a message to his Radical colleagues predicting that 'tomorrow all of you will have to join me'. They had walked out of the Chamber of Deputies after Sammartino's expulsion. But that had simply opened the way for a field day of Congressional rubber-stamping. Without so much as looking at the mimeographed budget report on their desk, the Perónista deputies passed a £425 million budget, then whipped through 28 bills in four hours, one of which gave the President dictatorial rights to govern by decree whenever he felt the nation's welfare demanded it. Another allowed him to gaol anyone who showed 'disrespect' for any official from President to dog-catcher.

But when the Perónistas turned their attention to yet another bill authorising a convention to amend the country's 1853 constitution, the Radicals hurried back to the Chamber for a last ditch battle to salvage some remnants of Argentina's badly tattered democracy. They attacked the Government for railroading the reform bill through the Congress before the country had a chance to study it. 'We are watching the destruction of Parliament,' cried Radical Deputy Alfredo R. Vitolo. Another Radical shouted: 'We want reform for the people and not for the President.' From 4 o'clock in the afternoon until 2.50 the next morning the opposition fought a futile delaying action. Then the bill was passed. One of its provisions, once a constitutional convention ratified it, enabled Perón to succeed himself as President, a step that brought a warning from the Radicals that the country was heading towards a situation where 'all political, economic, and cultural powers' would be concentrated under 'one official party and its chief'. The warning reached few Argentines. The Government-controlled press and radio saw to that.

But a few old enemies of Evita decided to register their protest against the constitutional changes. On Calle Florida — probably the most famous shopping street in South America — a group of the wealthiest and most socially prominent women in Argentina paraded with banners and chanted 'Save the Constitution'. It was an unlikely sight, a huddled group of fur-coated elderly and middle-aged ladies all looking a little scared at their temerity. But outside the opposition newspaper *La Nacion* they sang the national anthem with its chorus line of *Libertad! Libertad! Libertad!*, and immediately were surrounded by hundreds of cheering shoppers. It was that kind of street, not the sort of place, with its high prices, that was likely to attract Evita's descamisados. But the cheering and the singing of the society ladies quickly attracted the attention of a police riot squad. Seven women were arrested, two of them Uruguayan tourists, a mother and daughter who had been shopping on Calle Florida and had stopped to watch the demonstration. All of them were thrown in gaol overnight and released the next morning with a scolding from the judge. But that was not the end of the matter. Evita had been out of town. When she returned and found out what had happened she immediately ordered that the women be re-arrested.

They were herded into cells reserved for prostitutes, a cruelly vindictive touch by Evita. She had done it before to a group of teenage girls who had been arrested for laughing at the rustic accent of a Perónista provincial governor while he was making a speech at the annual Rural Show, always one of the main social events of the year in Argentina because of its connection with the country's landed aristocracy. Evita knew exactly what horror and indignation that punishment would arouse in a society which set such a high premium on a girl's virtue. So she repeated it with the older women and then had them appear before a Perón-appointed judge who sentenced them to 30 days in jail, although one of them, who was 72 years old, was allowed to serve her sentence at home.

That evening, the Perónista paper *La Epoca* devoted most of its front page to condemning the women for seeking deliberately to embarrass the Government outside the country. 'The people will scourge their enemies,' the paper thundered. 'Traitors to the nation will not be tolerated.' Indeed, the Peróns seemed determined to make an example of the women. Possibly it was part of Evita's revenge against the Sociedad de Beneficiencia, for all five of the Argentine women involved were members. The Uruguayan Government tried but failed to persuade the Argentines to release the two Uruguayan women. As for the others, the Perónista majority in Congress made sure there would not be any public debate by the simple expedient of staying away from the Chamber until the women had finished serving their sentences. And to make sure that everybody got the point that opposition was no longer tolerated in Argentina, Perón growled that he recognised 'the inalienable right of an outworn oligarchy to a final kicking fit in its death agony. But even within that right, they should learn that if we so wish, we shall bind them securely so that they can kick no more.'

The next day, an underground edition of the banned Socialist weekly *Vanguardia* appeared on the streets of Buenos Aires with a particularly apt cartoon by its celebrated cartoonist Tristan. It showed Perón in full uniform, armed with club, knives, cannon, spear, bombs, rope, moneybag, and microphone. He was addressing a gagged figure, tied hands and feet to a stake and labelled 'opposition'. 'Stop bragging and come out and fight,' the General said in the cartoon. 'You cannot frighten me, you traitor, oligarch, thief, cheat, faker, and liar.'

While porteños giggled privately, the Peróns sent out the federal police on yet another dragnet hunt for the gadfly weekly. It had infuriated them both so often with its scathing personal attacks that they had closed it down but in the way that they normally dealt with their enemies — by bending laws to suit their purpose. Three charges had been brought against *Vanguardia* — its printing presses violated a municipal anti-noise measure, a weapon chosen by the Peróns with cool irony since the anti-noise ordinance had been sponsored some years back by the Socialists; its loading of papers into delivery trucks tied up traffic on the street; and its pressroom lacked proper first-aid equipment.

La Vanguardia's management said it would stop printing at

night and avoid loading during hours when the traffic was heavy, though it pointed out that several Perónista papers on the same street ran their presses after sundown without official rebuke. The paper also said it would see to it that the pressroom was well supplied with necessary first-aid equipment. But it was no use. The paper was forced to go underground, skipping from one secret printing plant to another, sometimes publishing on wrapping paper. Cartoonist Tristan found a special delight in laughing at Evita's flowery speeches with their constant references to the 'heart of Perón' and the 'heart of Evita'. He drew her bejewelled with a blank face and a heart-shaped mouth as her only identification.

No one who met Evita ever forgot her. Milton Bracker, who covered Argentina for the *New York Times* during her years of power, remembered a woman of incredible humourlessness, startling energy, and corroding rancour, who had an absolute inability to forget or forgive. In cold print, her speeches failed to convey the constant sense of offended righteousness in her voice; the fusion of tension and outrage which may have had a deeper effect upon her listeners than her words; and the semi-mystic, fear-ridden role which made her probably the most idolised, hated and mistrusted woman in the world in her day. Her temper was notorious. A high-ranking diplomat once heard her in the presence of other high officials scream at Argentina's Minister of the Treasury: 'Shut up Cereijo, shut up!' And yet she could speak gently and lovingly over the radio at midnight on Christmas Eve to her 'beloved descamisados'.

But it was on the balcony that Evita reigned supreme. It has always been the podium of Latin American demagogues. Ecuador's popular populist Jose Maria Velasco Ibarra, who was regularly elected President and deposed just as often, once cried from exile: 'Give me a balcony in each town and I shall take possession of Ecuador.' Juan and Eva Perón had that same spellbinding appeal for working-class Argentines. Indeed, the ardour of the vast crowds that packed Plaza de Mayo never seemed to dim with the passing of the years. Whether the Peróns were celebrating an anniversary, like October the 17th, or seeking reassurance in a time of crisis, Argentines would turn out by the tens of thousands, waving aloft banners and pictures of their hero and heroine along with shirts tied to poles, the symbol of the descamisado.

After hours of noise, the singing of Perónista songs and the chanting of slogans, rising to a crescendo of 'Evita! Evita! Perón! Perón!' the President and his wife like actors on a cue, would fling open the big windows and walk out on to the balcony. The script rarely changed. Perón spoke first. He only had time to say: 'shirtless companions' and the crowd instantly interrupted with shouts of 'the coat, the coat'. Perón would laugh, take off his coat, and in shirt-sleeves launch into his speech. His powerful voice thundered through the plaza, deafening the ears of those who stood too close to the loudspeakers. His words poured out with a rhythm, the tempo building, slackening, pausing, at which point the uninitiated, the first-timers, applauded like a concert-goer confusing the end of a movement for the end of the symphony. Then, with a flourish and a cry of *companeros descamisados*', he would be off again.

As he finished, the chant went up: 'Evita, Evita', and the slim, tiny figure with burning eyes and blonde hair, wrapped in mink and glittering with diamonds, stepped forward to the micro-phones, her arms outstretched to the people below. She spoke faster than Perón, whipping her audience with the shrillness of her voice into a frenzy of loyalty and devotion. As always, she humbled herself before the man she publicly worshipped as a wise, benign, semi-divine king. 'He is a god to us,' she cried. 'We cannot conceive of heaven without Perón. He is our sun, our air, our water, our life. I want nothing but to be the heart of Perón. Because though I do my best to understand him and learn his marvellous ways, whenever he makes a decision, I barely mumble. Whenever he speaks, I hardly utter a single word. Whenever he gives advice, I scarcely dare make a suggestion. What he sees I hardly glimpse. But I see him with the eyes of my soul . . . And I have pledged myself to collect the hopes of the Argentine people and empty them in the marvellous heart of Perón so that he may turn them into realities.' Then she turned to her husband. 'The humble people, my General, have come here to prove, as they have always done, that the miracle that happened 2,000 years ago is happening again. The rich, the learned, the men in power never understood Christ. It was the humble and the poor who understood, because their souls, unlike the souls of the rich, are not sealed up with avarice and selfishness.' Down below the crowd roared their agreement: 'Uno-dos-tres-quatro/tenemos Perón para rato' — one, two three, four/We want Perón for evermore.

If Evita's words sounded close to heresy in a country as catholic as Argentina, then so be it as far as she was concerned.

In her autobiography she wrote: 'God who could not conceive heaven without his mother, whom he liked so much, will forgive me because my heart cannot conceive it without Perón . . . I am certain that, by imitating Christ, Perón feels a deep love for humanity and that this, more than anything else, makes him great, magnificently great.'

No one who knew her doubted she meant it with every taut muscle in her tiny body. There was a mysticism, a ferocious fanaticism about her, and she admitted it. 'I have dedicated myself fanatically to Perón and Perón's ideals,' she often said. 'Without fanaticism one cannot accomplish anything.' And she would chide those around her who didn't display it. 'We don't want shame-faced Perónistas; we do not want political neuters,' was her constant refrain. Her husband, more tolerant and relaxed, seemed content to allow her to pursue her ambitions. At the start of his Presidency, he had given her a desk and few chores to do at the Ministry of Labour. Within two years she was virtually running the country.

She controlled her own political army of five million workers, her descamisados, members of the General Confederation of Labour, the CGT. Its General Secretary, Jose Espejo, a squat, black-moustached little man, had been the hall porter in her old Calle Posadas apartment when she plucked him out to become her trade union push button. As an intimation of what his function would be, he remained silent during the press conference to announce his appointment while Evita answered all the questions. From then on he spent most of his time, not at CGT headquarters, but at the Labour Ministry where he was at the Señora's beck and call. She ruled the unions through him. Those that failed to cooperate did not get pay rises. They were closed down, their leaders jailed, replaced by brand new unions led by hand-picked Evita henchmen, the fate of the office workers union in Cordoba, the municipal workers' union in Buenos Aires, and the farm truckers' union.

The taxi drivers of Buenos Aires had been members of an anarcho-syndicalist union that had a history of telling Argentine governments to go to hell. They tried it with Evita. She formed an opposition union, put pro-Perón drivers at the wheel of opposition cabs. When the anarcho-syndicalists still resisted her embrace, the Government instituted petrol rationing and issued cards only to members of the pro-Perón union. Within a few weeks all the cab drivers were members of Evita's union. They were then able to share in the very real benefits — doubled, often trebled wages, paid holidays, bonuses, rest homes, and holiday camps — which CGT workers were enjoying for the very first time in Argentine history, thanks to their benefactress.

To those five million workers who would for ever worship Evita, she added four million women, liberated by her from shackles of their traditional subservient place in Latin society. They had possessed few rights, civil or political, until then. In the words of one angry, bitter feminist of the time, they were 'intellectually deadened by the actions of a society which thinks it dangerous . . . for them to be able to read and write . . . strongly dominated by religious beliefs, moulded by archaic prejudices, impregnated by a spirit so Spanish that it led man to treat woman with gallantry and at the same time to deny her personality; to value her grace and her beauty but to exploit her weakness and her ignorance, and to have no confidence in her intelligence; to fight a duel when he thought his own woman offended . . . but to shower any woman he passed in the streets with insolent remarks.' Those were exactly the prejudices that Evita had fought all her life.

'Because I have seen that women have never had material or spiritual opportunities — only poetry took them into account — and because I have known that women were a moral and spiritual resource in the world,' she said, 'I have placed myself at the side of all women of my country to struggle resolutely with them not only for the vindication of ourselves but also of our homes, our children, and our husbands.'

First she had to convince her husband who had lived for half a century without ever having shown any deviation from normal Argentine macho attitudes. In fact, his 1943 revolution had issued a stern call to the nation's womenfolk to concentrate on family life. For it was a period when office jobs, particularly in government ministries, had just begun to open up for women. But the military government summarily put an end to that. Indeed, such were the attitudes that President Farrell could indignantly complain that demonstrations against the government had been led by 'persons of the opposite sex who impeded the work of the police, exploiting the circumstance that the latter were gentlemen.'

With Perón's old-fashioned charm, there's little doubt that he would have echoed Farrell's shocked grumble. But Evita apparently changed all that. When he became President, she saw to it that woman's suffrage stood high on the list of the government's legislative programme. But there were plenty of Argentines, Perónistas among them, who showed a marked lack of enthusiasm for the prospect of emancipated women turning their way of life upside-down. The suffrage bill somehow seemed to linger in Congressional committees while other bills speeded through. So, shortly after Evita returned from her European tour, she marched into Congress and told the deputies that she would not leave until the bill had passed. With the Chamber's gallery packed with women and thousands more outside surrounding the building, the shaken legislators quickly did as they were told. Two days later, one hundred thousand Perónistas flocked into Plaza de Mayo to hear Perón promulgate the new law and to hear Evita assure the women, as well as the men, that a new era had dawned for Argentina.

The next step was to mobilise the power she had unleashed. On July 26, 1949, Evita brought into being the Perónista Feminist Party. As always now in Argentina, her presence completely dominated the packed Cervantes Theatre in Buenos Aires where 1,500 women had gathered. They were uninterested in the introductory remarks by the only man present, Governor Domingo Mercante of Buenos Aires Province. But they burst into wild cheering with cries of 'Evita! Evita!' when she arrived, wearing a business-like grey suit with black velvet collar and carrying a red-lined briefcase. She spoke for two hours, her words constantly interrupted by chants of 'Our lives for Evita'. She was named President of the Party, of course, and she took all the other executive offices as well. Within days, party offices were springing up all across the country. Even in the smallest of towns, the clubhouse of the Perónista Feminist Party was instantly recognisable by the giant portrait of Evita, bathed at night in neon-light, her face graciously inclined, a gentle smile on her lips.

But her hold over the Argentine people went much deeper than the women who owed her their vote or the workman his latest wage increase. It had everything to do with what her enemies called the most gigantic protection racket-cum-slush fund the world had ever seen — her Social Aid Foundation. She had started it with £500 of her own money to compete against the charity run by the haughty, aristocratic dowagers she hated so bitterly. Within three years their charity had vanished because the government, at Evita's behest, had cut off the subsidy which had been its principal means of support. In the same period, her foundation's income soared to £50 million a year and had become the country's biggest single enterprise.

Every person in Argentina — ambassadors, chambermaids, multi-millionaires — contributed 'voluntarily' to the fund. Members of the CGT, controlled by Evita, gave her two days of their pay each year. There was such a howl of protest from the volunteers in the first year that Treasury Minister Ramon Cereijo announced that the foundation would return the money. But at the same time word was leaked that a hurt and angry Evita would be thinking twice about granting any more union pay rises. By magic, the protests ceased and CGT General Secretary Espejo at a special ceremony in the Ministry of Labour told Evita that the country's workers had unanimously refused to take their money back. Graciously, she told him that she accepted their 'magnificent gesture', adding that 'I had expected no less from my beloved descamisados. I accept their contribution with profound emotion.' From then on she also accepted a percentage of the wage increases she awarded them, making the rise retrospective for one month with half of that month's increase going to her foundation. The unions also fell over themselves to make special fund-raising contributions to keep in her good graces — £334,500 from the railway workers, £195,125 from the municipal workers, £167,250 from the tramcar workers.

Evita also creamed 20 per cent off the top of the national lottery. She received millions of pesos of public funds in the form of state contributions authorised by the Perónist-controlled Congress. Big business gave generously, too, after firms discovered the penalty for not doing so. The Massone Institute, one of South America's leading manufacturers of bio-chemicals, refused to contribute to the foundation because Arnaldo Massone, the company's president, loathed the Peróns and was not prepared to give a single peso to Evita Perón. Under pressure he still refused. Retribution was swift. He and other directors of the company were indicted on charges of falsifying the chemical inscriptions of a number of biochemical products. They were sentenced to three months' imprisonment and the institute was fined £13,567. As was usual in such cases, the police gave Arnoldo Massone sufficient time to pack his bags and flee across the river to join the growing band of Argentine refugees.

They were soon followed by the directors of the Mu Mu sweet company. She had asked them for 100,000 packets of sweets. They sent an emissary with a message offering to sell them at cost. Back came the reply that she expected them free. When they refused, a government inspector appeared at the factory. His report, published in all the Perónista newspapers, stated that he had found rat hairs in the caramel mixture. The factory was closed and a heavy fine was imposed on the company for operating an unhygienic plant. The judge who handled the case thoughtfully passed the proceeds of the fine on to the foundation. After that, whenever one of Evita's collectors visited a company that was proving difficult, he simply took out a sweet from his pocket and chewed reflectively in front of the directors. He rarely had to make a return visit.

There never was any accounting for the money. Fleur Cowles, wife of an American publishing tycoon, visited Evita in the Casa Rosada, and asked her how she kept track on the money pouring into the foundation's coffers. 'I put the question to her carefully, saying I presumed she kept a very strict accounting of every dollar spent. "How else will history give you credit for your charitable efforts?" was the way I put it. She brushed history and the accountants aside without blinking an eye. "Keeping books on charity is capitalistic nonsense," she said. "I just use the money for the poor. I can't stop to count it."'*

Just how much she siphoned off for herself no one will ever know — enough anyway to pay for her priceless collection of jewellery and to fill a number of Swiss bank accounts. But Argentina's poor certainly benefited in a way they never had before. She built them one thousand schools, poured millions into medical services that had never been available for the poor before. In fact, there were only 57 hospitals in the whole of Argentina when Perón came to power. By the end of 1949 there were 119, most of them bearing the imprint of the Eva Duarte de Perón Social Aid Foundation. Her nursing schools trained 1,300 nurses every year who went out into the slums and the countryside to staff the clinics that were being opened at a rate of one a week. She operated her own Red Cross, sending emergency aid and medical teams to the scene of disasters not only in Argentina but throughout Latin America. After the 1949 Ecuador earthquake which killed 800 people, Evita poured in relief — doctors, nurses, blood plasma, medical supplies, food, clothing. The young state of Israel received shipments of food and clothing for its immigrants. So did a Washington charity, much to the embarrassment of Americans.

*From Bloody Precedent *by Fleur Cowles.*

115

She built homes for unmarried mothers, homes for the aged, parks and recreation centres, whole holiday resorts by the sea for workers. There was a hotel for working girls arriving homeless in the Big City for the first time, just like Evita not so many years before. She built orphanages for the 'thousands of little ones, without schooling, without hygienic care, without any home life, herded together in sordid huts and falling ready prey to illnesses of every kind.' At Christmas time she remembered her own deprived childhood. Through the foundation, every post office in the country gave away a bottle of cider, a loaf of traditional sweet bread, and toys for every family that called in on Christmas Eve. Each package carried a picture of Evita and her husband with a Christmas greeting from them to their 'beloved descamisados'.

One of her great joys was a model children's village which she built in a Buenos Aires suburb. It contained small-scale houses, shops, a church and a bank, plus luxurious dormitories, dining rooms and playrooms. There were supposed to be at least 200 children between the ages of two and five living in the village. But it always seemed to be as deserted as a ghost town whenever Evita took guests there from abroad, which she loved to do. Sniffed Fleur Cowles after Evita had given her the grand tour: 'It reminded me of a set for a ballet — not for human occupancy. Quantities of expensive toys, most of them bigger than any occupants, were arranged carefully in corridors, in playrooms, in bedrooms. But they seemed nailed to their positions; certainly they were never to be moved by children at play. Beautifully hand-made little dresses and coats were dusty on their hangers in the bedroom closets which Evita opened so proudly to show me. The beds were almost totally untouched. No children scampered through the toy houses, shops, library and school through which Evita trailed us; our heads stooped to squeeze inside the miniature buildings set on the front lawns. "All the children are out on a huge picnic today," Evita explained.' Another visitor, a diplomat's wife, commented afterwards: 'It's the wish fulfillment of a little girl who had never had a doll's house of her own.'

Wish fulfillment it may have been. But the schools, hospitals, clinics, orphanages were not so easy to sneer away. As one of the more intelligent of her enemies remarked: 'If we had done for the workers a tiny fraction of what Evita had done, there never would have been a Perón and she would still be a bad actress.' But they had not. Indeed, no one else had the right to say as she did, proudly, that 'I spend every hour of the day looking after the needs of the descamisados to show them that here, in the Argentine Republic . . . the gulf which had separated the people from the government no longer exists.'

The routine of her life never changed unless she was out of town. Up at 5.30, breakfast with her husband at 6.30, audiences in the residence at 8.00, in her office at the Ministry of Labour by mid-morning. It looked out over Hipolíto Irigoyen Street, only a few blocks from the Casa Rosada. Four vases filled with fresh flowers daily stood on a long mahogany table against the wall. There were three telephones on it as well, one of them ivory coloured — a direct line to her husband in the Palace. It was a small room, 15 feet long by 10 feet wide, with a sofa and three easy chairs, not that anyone ever seemed to sit down in them. For Evita usually spent her morning flitting from reception room to reception room in the Ministry, meeting delegations that poured in throughout the day from around the country. For each there was a battery of photographers, one of them from her own newspaper, *Democracia*, which published eight pictures of Evita on the average each day, and reaching as many as 25 on her return from Europe.

On one random morning, she saw the Workers' Association of the National Grain Elevator Commission, Labour and Social Organisation of the Indoor Workers of the Jockey Club, Society of Cinema Cashiers, Workers' Protective Association of the National Schools, Food Workers' Union of Buenos Aires, Lithuanian Catholic Association, and the Argentine Musicians' Federation. By then her personal secretary, Isabel Ernst, was trying to rush her home for lunch with her husband. He looks after her very carefully. She works so hard. But he insists that she eat regularly. He's been waiting for her for luncheon since 12.15, and, look, it is now 12.45. He gets very impatient.'

Both she and Perón usually took a long midday break. But at around 5 o'clock, she would be on her way back to the Ministry to play her greatest role, that of Lady Bountiful. Milton Bracker of the *New York Times* was there one afternoon and sent his newspaper a fascinating report of her performance:

'Two policemen guard the entrance to the Ministry, which the Señora has in effect taken over from the Minister himself. Colour posters of both Peróns deck the crowded lobby. Evita has two offices which adjoin but do not connect. Into one, poor mothers and children are screened on the basis of slips of paper fixing their audience for 4 pm. Into the other filter better dressed

117

callers invited for special audiences at 5 pm. The *Presidenta*'s car rolls up a little after 5.30 and Evita slips into the latter room via a side door.

'The office is scarcely less crowded than the hallway. Yet many of those waiting are important people: the Governor of Buenos Aires Province, the wife of the Minister of Education, a distinguished Italian actor. Evita's technique is like that of a chess master, playing twenty-five simultaneous games at high speed. She walks from one to another, listening briefly, though with apparent intentness, speaking rapidly with quick gestures and frequent smiles which flash her teeth.

'Her voice rises as she rebuts a complaint about a benefit concert. ("In this matter, Gigli is an authority. He knows what he's doing.") She tells a banker that whoever gets a certain job must be very suave, very patient. She calls peremptorily for the head of the General Labour Confederation (Jose Espejo). She sends a publicist away glowing with the idea he'd make a fine counsellor of the embassy in Washington. And she pats the Governor of Buenos Aires and guides him back to an impatient circle by the window, where small talk is running thin.

'She parries a question about her personal reaction to her work.

'"All these people, you see?" she says. "I am nothing — my work is everything."

'She is off on another swing. When she returns, there is a little more fencing and she extends a soft, warm, hand, smiling superbly.

'"Time is my greatest enemy," she says.

'Meanwhile the other room overflows with children. They squirm and giggle, scramble on the floor and wail. At about 6.15, a premature murmur goes around. "*Ya viene!*" ("Here she comes!") Presently the Señora steps in briskly. She sits beneath a huge oil of "Amalia", a melancholy lady in black mantilla, by Juan Carlos Alonso. Other pictures in the red-damasked room are of the Peróns or of Christ.

'Four secretaries surround the table. The synchronisation is like that of an operating room. One shoves a pencil into her hand, another readies a pad of clothing tickets, a third holds up a 'phone.

'Señora Perón speaks animatedly. "Yes, yes. We are very grateful to you. If there is anything else you need, let us know. *Hasta luego*." Most of the people in the room listen dumbly. A stringy-haired mother rocks her child.

118

The first supplicant is a shapeless woman with a toil-worn face. The First Lady turns her brown eyes; clusters of black crystals tinkle at the brim of her open-crown straw.

'"I live in one room," the woman says. "I want a house to live in . . ."

"How many children do you have?"

'"Eight."

'The *Presidenta* murmurs to one of her secretaries.

'"We can provide a wooden house," she begins. The woman asks questions. Evita is dictating. "Clothing for nine . . . a large bed, complete . . ." She turns for a brief aside to a visiting Ambassador. Then she takes the slip from the secretary's pad and signs "E.P." The woman shuffles out with the slip.

'Señora Perón distributes clothing, bedding, furniture, drugs and fifty-peso notes (about ten dollars). The drug is usually streptomycin. There is no indication as to why the patient actually needs it. But Evita says "four grams," and the public health secretary writes it out. The fifty peso notes come from a seemingly endless supply under the blotter. All are new and folded in half. Evita doles them out one or two at a time. No account is kept and Evita told me in a written answer, "None will be." The foundation is not a "business proposition."

'Gradually the clutter of children thins. A priest from a distant province speaks urgently. "An audience for the padre at the residence on Monday at 8," says Evita, rising as the audience ticket is written.

'She poses with the visiting Ambassador, who contributes 100,000 pesos (£2,500). As she leaves for an *acto* or public ceremony, a young man looks on disappointedly. "Monday," she tells him, sweetly rueful.

'She sweeps across the amphitheatre. A thousand-odd graphic arts workers cheer. The stirring words of the national anthem move lightly over her lips. Another acto follows. When Evita leaves after four hours, everyone else is exhausted. On Wednesdays the scene shifts to the Casa Rosada, where she and her Juancito put on the act together.'

In the evening, she was usually out again, for another acto. Fleur Cowles accompanied her one night to the Opera House in Buenos Aires. The audience literally hung from the rafters; so many streamers and flags curled from each hand that the great tiered circle looked like a splashed gilt crazyquilt. Women and their children, ignoring the hour, were packed inside each box, crowding the edges. Everyone was yelling, throwing flowers and

119

waving a little blue-and-white flag with Evita emblazoned on it.

'As Evita's car entered the Opera square, the calm of the night turned to pandemonium. The darkened streets through which we had been driven in Evita's bullet-proof car had been quiet and deserted, until we turned a corner into dense crowds. Police strained to form an opening wedge for her car. All that this pressing mass of humanity really wanted was to surge towards Evita. Those nearest Evita, at the entrance, did break police lines to plunge at her, to touch her skirt, to see, at close hand, the Cinderella dressed by Dior, with her three-quarters of a million dollars in jewels. It was an orgy of curiosity and admiration.

'The occasion was the handing out of pensions to workers over seventy . . . On the big empty stage was a handful of gnarled, quivering old men summoned to receive her bounty. They sat in a Breughel-like, half-lit semi-circle against the back wall, silent and frightened. Thousands and thousands had come to see Evita distribute largesse and to hear her speak. They came to admire Evita, and, if luck would have it, to cash in on an extraordinary lottery.

'The game is childlike: everyone throws a little folded sheet of paper with his name and address written on it towards Evita whenever she makes a public appearance. Thousands of tiny folded papers fluttered through the Opera House during the proceedings that night.

'Whenever Evita stoops to pick up such a paper, that gesture means the winning of the "sweepstakes" for the lucky person whose name is on the crumpled missile. An audience with Evita in her Social Aid Foundation automatically follows.'

But to Evita, it was no sweepstakes or charity, as others called it. There was a difference, she always insisted, between the charity of the wealthy dowagers and the social assistance of her foundation. 'Charity humiliates and social aid dignifies and stimulates,' she said. 'Charity is given discreetly; social aid rationally. Charity prolongs the situation; social aid solves it . . . Charity is the generosity of the fortunate; social aid remedies social inequalities. Charity separates the wealthy from the poor; social aid raises the needy to the level of the well-to-do.' Her foundation, she always claimed, had emerged to cope with the conditions in which millions of Argentines lived 'with starvation wages, without security of employment, without rights to self-improvement, without a single guarantee for themselves, their families, and their future.' So while her enemies regarded her as beneath contempt, a charlatan, thief, demagogue, those other Argentines really did believe that she was the *Dama de la Esperanza*, the Lady of Hope.

10

TEETHING TROUBLES

In June of 1950, on one of those grey Argentine winter days when the wind whips off the River Plate and blows with a bitter fierceness through the streets of Buenos Aires, a new batch of posters plastered the downtown walls of the city with an unseasonal splash of colour and a message: 'Eva Perón, standard bearer of the meek, should be elected in 1952.' Elected for what? The posters did not elaborate, although it was already being taken for granted by most people in Argentina that Evita would choose to run as the Vice-Presidential candidate on her husband's ticket for another six years in office. Had she now decided to aim even higher? In wealthy porteño circles, where even the mere mention of that woman's name was considered a social faux pas, the possibility was too intriguing to be ignored. She had the power. Did she now want the office, too?

It was the kind of speculation that fed the rumour mills of the Buenos Aires cocktail circuit with tales of matrimonial troubles in the Casa Rosada. But they were usually embroidered versions of old stories that had done the rounds before. There was certainly no evidence to indicate there was truth in any of them. On the contrary, the Peróns seemed very happy. In many ways theirs was an ideal marriage. They had clawed their way to the top together. They ran the country together. They complemented each other; his sophistication and avuncular charm blunting the raw cutting edge of her political passion; she driving him on to defend commitments he might not have made without her backbone and strength to support him. Like the Emperor Justinian and Theodora, also an actress and the most beautiful woman in Byzantium, whom Justinian married and enthroned as co-ruler, the Peróns never wavered in their love for each other as they rode the roller-coaster of political power.

It often showed in public. On one occasion, when Perón was inaugurating Evita's children's village, he praised her so highly that tears welled in her eyes. With a grin, he stopped talking and turned and kissed her. 'These two tears,' he said, 'point to the great merit in this work, namely human emotion.' He was so obviously proud of her that he never missed an opportunity of letting everybody know it. 'You see her extraordinary influence — why is it? Is it because she dresses well and is pretty? No. She is loved and respected and honoured by all the humble because she cannot eat or sleep or live for doing good.' Whenever she left him on one of her frequent trips out into the provinces, he would bid her farewell with old-fashioned courtesy, bowing ceremoniously, then kissing her on the forehead. There was a charm and warmth about him, which she lacked. Her hero-worshipping praise of him in public was so extravagant it often verged on the ridiculous. But there is also no doubting the look of devotion shining from her eyes in 30-year-old photographs of the two of them together. And there was a day a year before she died when in a moment of crisis the brittle smile collapsed and she burst into tears, her shoulders heaving as she buried herself in his bear-like hug of protection.

They led a quiet life together. As they were always up so early in the morning, they rarely went out in the evening, except to official functions. Occasionally they had friends in for dinner and Perón would bound down the steps himself to open their guests' car door. Perhaps because they were both country-bred (or maybe because they had no children), they loved to have animals around them. Evita had two or three poodles, and the household also included two deer, two gazelles, and an amiable blackbird which perched on the General's shoulder. There were even more animals out at their 45-acre country home in San Vicente, a distant suburb of Buenos Aires. Perón's brother Mario was director of the city's zoological gardens. So naturally they had their pick of animals — fifteen ostriches, eight storks, two flamingos, five llamas, and eleven *chajas*, a native bird.

Evita loved her weekend home (called a *quinta* in Argentina because it is never more than 50 kilometres from town). She wore slacks there, which provoked much tut-tutting and 'I-told-you-so's' among fashion-conscious Argentine ladies, while Perón became a weekend gaucho in baggy pants. Whenever they had guests, he appointed himself the *asador*, the barbecue chef, while she baked *empanadas* (meat pies) in her own *criollo* native oven. She put on a little weight in those early days. There were signs of a double chin, indications that the Ibarguren family plumpness was waiting to burst out of that trim figure. But it never happened. Strict adherence to diet and the frantic pace of her life kept her slim from then on.

Evita had changed a great deal over the years. A curly-haired brunette wearing frilly blouses and too much lipstick in her early days in Buenos Aires, she had become a reddish-blonde by the time she moved into the Presidential Residence in 1946. She wore clothes that showed off her fine figure, luxurious gowns cut low. At that time they were a little too loud and elaborate, and she wore too much jewellery. But the trip to Europe transformed her. She started spending over £10,000 a year on exquisite Paris clothes designed by Dior, Fath and Balmain. Then, as she became the most dominating personality in the land, so her appearance changed again. She was now the brisk, efficient career woman, wearing simple conservative suits, her blonde hair tied back in an old-fashioned bun.

Fleur Cowles was surprised at her appearance when she met her for the first time in July 1950. 'She was not at all the flashy companion old news accounts prepared you for . . . a trim, obviously busy woman, with an air that was efficient, aware, composed. Except for her jewels, at first glance she even looked modest. She was elegantly dressed in a navy-blue suit by Jacques Fath; she had an expensive navy-blue velvet beret on her blonde hair. There were sables on her arm; she wore them as if she had always carried them. She was dressed as millions of women would like to be dressed. The only give-away was the orchid in her lapel. No real flower, that, but one of diamonds, larger even than an orchid, about 5 inches across by 7 inches high — a brooch of big, pure white diamonds that must have been worth $250,000. Barrel earclips of diamond baguettes and her ball-like diamond ring were minor accessories by contrast.'

'She stared back at me at first with a cold, unpleasant look.' But 'after she'd taken in every part of me (including the black pearl and diamond pin I wore),' Evita asked Fleur to stay a while. 'She displayed a willingness (later, eagerness) to talk "girl talk" about clothes, jewelry, coiffure. . . She kept eyeing the jewel I wore. Perón winked at me and said in his halting English: "That's one she can't have." ' When Fleur remarked that Evita's hair was 'very becoming worn straight and simply, she asked if I would look at pictures of her in the many ways she had worn it during the years, then tell her if she was doing it the best way. Someone was sent off to bring her a range of her best photographs; they were laid out on the floor on the Napoleonic room. Full-length paintings of Evita and Perón stared at us from the walls, one with Evita's hair dressed in the bad sausage pompadour she originally wore as First Lady. I agreed heartily she looked her best in the newer, neater way she wore her hair that evening. I'm not sure Perón agreed, although that constant smile of his was ready.'

The cost of Evita's jewels, which she bought from Van Cleef and Arpels in Paris, hardly came out of her husband's pocket. His presidential salary was only £40 a week. Even the profits from the three newspapers she owned could not have supported her collection which had become so vast that she could match all her costumes with sets of diamonds, emeralds, and sapphires. She delighted in wearing them in the most poverty-stricken of city slums, knowing full well that part of her appeal to her followers was her Cinderella rags-to-riches success story. 'I am taking the jewels from the oligarchs for you,' she told them. 'One day you'll inherit the whole collection.'

On that basis, she no doubt rationalised that she could finance her Paris purchases through her foundation, as she never tired of pointing out that it was the duty of social aid to 'raise the needy to the level of the well-to-do.' How she did it certainly never seemed to bother her husband. One day, while showing a visitor over the Residence, he opened closet after closet of Evita's clothes. 'Not exactly a descamisada, eh?' he grinned. No one in the Party apparently minded (if they did, they had the sense to keep quiet about it) and as for political enemies, they did not count. It was simply accepted that like the blonde in *Gentlemen Prefer Blondes*, Evita believed that 'kissing your hand may make you feel very very good but a diamond and sapphire bracelet last forever.' Accordingly, the taxi drivers' union gave her a diamond watch one year for her birthday. The Perónista newspaper editors weighed in with diamond earrings, and the Cabinet split the cost among Ministers for a pearl and diamond necklace.

126

One opposition deputy, Colonel Atilio Cattaneo, did have the temerity to grumble about the thief who entered office poor but who would leave it rich and the Señora's relatives 'who were so poor in 1943 and now are multi-millionaires'. Perón was furious. Summoning fifty local and foreign reporters and the entire Cabinet to the Casa Rosada at 8.30 for his first press conference in almost four years, he announced that he felt obliged to 'set an example' to the rest of the country on what to do when falsely accused. 'A man holding office must look to his reputation,' he said. 'Now that I have been accused of robbing the public purse, I intend to show by documents that these charges are false. And since *Prensa* and *Nacion* have echoed these uncalled for calumnies, I now intend to see that these accusers are brought to justice.'

At this point, Perón who had entered the room wearing his usual broad smile had tears streaming down his cheeks. On the table lay a big white envelope. The envelope, said Perón, contained a statement listing his assets before he took office; it had been sealed for three years. He persuaded two American newsmen, Milton Bracker of the *New York Times* and William Horsey of the United Press news agency to open it. Then he called *Prensa* and *Nacion* reporters forward to sign statements attesting to the contents. The statement, dated July 6, 1946 (a month after Perón took office), said simply that his assets then consisted of the San Vicente quinta, a Packard and a share in his father's modest estate.

Of course, all this did not prove anything. What people wanted to know was not what Perón had in the way of assets when he took office but what he had acquired since then. No one dared ask that question, except Colonel Cattaneo. The Peronistas in Congress lifted his parliamentary immunity and a warrant was issued for his arrest on a charge of 'desacato' or disrespect to the President, a new law which had just come into effect. Police raided eighteen houses in Buenos Aires searching for him. But by then the Colonel had crossed the river to Uruguay.

There were a number of other things irritating the normally exuberant Juan Domingo Perón at the time. His teeth for one. His dentist had been a good friend, which is perhaps why Perón had overlooked the fact that he had once been arrested for practising without a licence. Returning from a trip to the USA, where he had been buying cars for top government officials,

Oliva Paz found the President's teeth in worse shape than ever. He lanced the gums. But that did nothing for his patient's terrible case of pyorrhoea. So Perón demanded to see a specialist. His Secretary of Education, Oscar Ivanissevich, a skilled surgeon who had taken out the President's appendix, recommended Professor Stanley D. Tylman of the University of Illinois, who had just arrived in Buenos Aires. Dr Tylman was willing to look at Perón's mouth. The examination went something like this:

Tylman (peering into Perón's mouth): 'You have one of the worst pyorrhoea cases I have ever seen. The treatment you have been receiving is incredibly bad.'

Oliva Paz (translating): 'Although you have one of the worst attacks of pyorrhoea I have ever seen, your gums have been very well treated.'

Tylman: 'Since your mouth has been so neglected and maltreated, there is no way to avoid extracting at least six teeth.'

Oliva Paz (still translating): 'With the fine treatment you have been getting, your mouth and gums will be alright within a few weeks.'

Although Perón spoke a little English, he had been listening attentively to the translation and on hearing the good news he gave one of his broad grins, pumped the professor's hand and said 'Thank you, thank you.' Dr Tylman realised immediately that something was wrong. He called in Ivanissevich to give a correct translation, then yanked out the six offending teeth. Perón was so delighted with the treatment that he and Evita invited the professor over to the Residence for dinner every night and then drove him out to the airport when he returned to the United States. As for Oliva Paz, he took the well travelled route across the river to Uruguay.

But embarrassing and painful as Perón's teething troubles were, they were nothing compared to the ego-shattering debacle of Argentina's entry into the world of atomic power. One day he matter-of-factly announced that his country had produced atomic energy. Naturally, the news made headlines around the world, placing Argentina in one verbal leap in the super-power league alongside the United States, the Soviet Union, and Great Britain. Perón's claim was that a team of Argentine physicists headed by an Austrian, Ronald Richter, had produced thermo-nuclear atomic reactions using energy from the sun instead of uranium.

Such incredulity was voiced by foreign scientists that Perón vented his anger in an interview with Evita's newspaper *Democracia*. 'I'm not interested in what the United States or any other country in the world thinks,' he thundered. 'I am only speaking to the Argentine people to whom I am responsible because I have always avoided the course followed by politicians and newspapers in other countries in the world who lie consciously, directing their lies to their own people and spreading them abroad. They have not yet told the first truth, while I have not yet told the first lie.' No one in Argentina, of course, was accusing the President of lying. To do so was to invite a year or two in jail for desacato, disrespect. Nevertheless, a few months later hoaxer Richter disappeared across the river to Uruguay, having squandered a few million dollars of Argentina's fast vanishing foreign exchange reserves.

Still, even the atomic caper was a minor misadventure compared with Perón's bungling of the nation's economy. At the end of World War II, Argentina's foreign exchange stood at over 500,000 million dollars, making it one of the richest countries in the world. The peso stood at four to the dollar and for every one of those pesos there was a backing of one and a half pesos in gold. Perón knew what he wanted to do with all that money, and his intentions were good. He was going to lift the nation's workers out of their feudal, impoverished bondage, rescue the country from its long servitude as an economic colony of the British, pay off the country's foreign debt, and build an industrial base so that Argentina would no longer be a nation of peasants at the mercy of the industrial world and its own land-wealthy oligarchs. He paved those intentions with the nation's gold, and by the late 1940s the gold was running out.

The problem was that Argentina simply did not have the foundations for an industrial economy. It had no coal or iron worth mentioning, produced less than half of the oil it needed, and did not have a large enough population (16 millions in 1947) to run both a great industrial plant and a great farm economy. The government paid farmers and stockmen low prices for their products and sold them abroad for high prices, using the profits to build up industry. For a while Argentina led the world in increased production. But this very success hurt the country's agriculture. Drawn by high wages and the attractions of urban life, hundreds of thousands of rural workers abandoned the farms for the squalid, overcrowded slums of the big cities. The population of Buenos Aires increased by a million in one year. Worse yet, nature added to the farmers' woes. For two years in a row, Argentina suffered from devastating droughts. The parched pampas, once rich in corn, wheat, and cattle, cracked and blew away in a cloud of dust. The editor of the economic journal, *The Review of the River Plate*, wrote: 'Last week I visited one of the western ranches in the south of Santa Fé province, and while there I saw part of the province of Cordoba blowing over in the form of a huge yellow cloud.'

With less grain and meat to sell abroad, Argentina received less foreign exchange with which to buy coal, oil, raw materials, and machinery. Industrial production fell, unemployment rose. Foreign exchange reserves melted away to nothing and the balance of trade turned against Argentina. For the first time in history, Argentina had to import wheat. There was even a scarcity of beef in Buenos Aires, the legendary beef capital of the world. For Juan Perón, for all Argentines, there could be no worse crisis than that. American writer Bernard Collier once claimed that the most distinctive quality about Buenos Aires is its *olor porteño* — the odour of fresh beef roasting.

'An Argentine must have fresh beef,' he wrote. 'Without fresh beef he feels weak, angry, anxious and hungry, all the time without satisfaction. Give him lamb and he can't stand the taste; chicken, fish and pork he rejects as baby food. You walk along a downtown street at 1 o'clock in the afternoon and watch the pipefitters, the cable splicers, the sewer workers, the diggers and the pavers pop out of holes in the street to check on the doneness of a 2-pound *bife*, which is sizzling over a wood or charcoal fire on a grill fashioned out of a tar bucket and iron reinforcing rods. By 2 o'clock on a hot summer afternoon there will be workmen in blue shirts and leather sandals lolling in the shade of buildings or construction fences all over town. In the winter they will be hunched over the little fires. They will be sleepy with their big steak and most of a bottle of good red wine and half a loaf of crusty Italian bread inside. At 3 o'clock they will return to their jobs refreshed and strong again. When they get home at night they want another steak for supper.'

Businessmen in the skyscrapers, the shopkeepers and the gaucho on the pampas feel the same way. They want their beef every day, and when it is scarce, there is great unrest among Argentines across the land. So when porteños found themselves having to pay black-market prices for beef imported from Uruguay, even the Peróns' beloved descamisados began to grumble, although Evita continued to push wages up to keep them happy. But prices now were rising just as fast. The four peso dollar of 1945 had become the 16 peso dollar of 1949, a fact that the General tried to brush away with the comment that he did not care if the peso was worthless outside Argentina because 'I don't have to buy anything abroad.'

If his most loyal supporters believed that, even they must have found it hard to swallow his claim that he had been examining dustbins on his way to the Casa Rosada each morning. The result of his investigation, he said, was that the amount of bread and meat thrown away each day would feed another city as large as Buenos Aires. There was plenty for everybody, he said firmly, if wasteful Argentines would eat what was on their plate instead of throwing it away.

But there were plenty of Argentines who were not amused by the rhetoric. The army, for one, saw a chance of settling old scores with the traitor who had trumped his military colleagues' machine guns in 1945 with his descamisados. In the summer of 1949, rumours flooded Buenos Aires that the army had demanded the retirement of Evita from public life. No one knew whether the rumours were true because all the newspapers in Buenos Aires were on strike. That in itself was odd, too. For by all Perónista rules, the strike of newspaper typographers should have been easy to settle. Their demand for a 25 percent pay rise to meet the soaring cost of living seemed mild enough by the standards that Evita had set for settlements in the past. The union's officers had taken their demands to her. But to their surprise, she only met them halfway and then lectured them on the need for economic responsibility. They backed down, as union bosses usually did when in confrontation with the Señora. But to everybody's surprise, the rank-and-file revolted. Evita promptly called in convicts from the federal prison in Buenos Aires as strikebreakers. But they refused to work, too. Within days, every newspaper in Buenos Aires, including her own *Democracia*, had shut down. And the rumours were in full spate.

11

REPRESSION

Normally, mid-summer is not a time for revolution in Argentina. The capital takes on a sleepy air. Small shops close for the holidays. Government offices work only half days, and most of the city moves to Mar del Plata, which is the Blackpool of South America. There were probably a few generals, headed by War Minister Humberto Sosa Molina, who were ready to pull a *golpe*, a revolution, right there and then in the summer of 1949. But they were handicapped by a lack of officers and men. Most of them were in Mar del Plata, too, lying out on their own two feet of beach, listening to Hector y Su Jazz Band at the world's largest casino, dining nightly on two inch-thick steaks, and tangoing to a new tune called 'El Cafetin de Buenos Aires' before losing a portion of their latest big pay increase at the roulette tables. Enfuriatingly for General Sosa Molina, a golpe at that particular moment, if he had been able to round up a few soldiers, would have met with little resistance. For thousands of the most fervent of descamisados were also at Mar del Plata in the big Government sea-front hotels that Evita's social aid foundation had built for them.

So the Minister had to settle for daily crisis meetings with the Peróns who were themselves on holiday at their San Vicente quinta. Sosa Molina told them bluntly that the army not only wanted Evita out of politics, it wanted her foundation closed and an end to bribery and corruption in the government. To show that the army meant business, the guard at Campo de Mayo, the big army encampment on the outskirts of the capital, refused to allow Evita on to the base when she called without an invitation. For a few days it appeared to be touch-and go as the Peróns fought for their political lives. He failed to turn up to open an international travel conference in Buenos Aires. She abruptly cancelled plans to speak at the Constitutional Convention which was meeting to replace the 1853 Constitution with one more to the liking of Perónistas.

When they did appear in public together, she spread her arms out in front of her and shook her head when the inevitable chant went up of 'Evita, Evita'. Right there and then, before a large outdoor crowd in Palermo Park in the city, Perón lashed out at the rumour-mongers. He said he had merely been resting in his San Vicente quinta and he'd had a good laugh with the messenger who told him that everybody believed he was a 'prisoner of his own government'. He assured his audience that he and Evita were 'perfectly calm and safe'. But in the newspaperless city, rumours continued to spread — Perón had offered to resign. Evita had chartered a plane to take her to Brazil.

But when the dust finally settled, it was the army that had lost once again. Infuriated by the treatment that his wife had received at Campo de Mayo, Perón angrily pointed out to his War Minister that his government had raised the pay of the rank and file soldier by a considerable amount, and his wife, through her foundation, had also bettered the lot of their families. So if the generals wanted to find out to whom the troops owed their loyalty, they should go ahead and try a golpe. That was the end of that.

But Evita wanted to make sure the generals were properly humiliated. She ordered them to invite her and her husband to lunch at Campo de Mayo at which the officers' wives had to be present. For many of them, it was the first time they had ever spoken to Eva Perón. They had to choke silently over their bifes as the War Minister humbled himself before her with a nation-wide radio audience gleefully listening in. 'The most worthy Señora of the most excellent President,' General Sosa Molina said, 'for her multiple activities to mitigate the troubles of her fellow beings and because she is enshrined in the hearts of the people, deserves all our sympathy and respectful consideration. The significance of her being among us as a special guest is none other than a stout denial of rumours that present the army as opposing her actions and thereby opposing the feelings of the people who support her.'

It was a moment of triumph for Evita, and she savoured it. A few days later, she was at the President's side when he took the oath to uphold the new constitution drawn up by the Perónista-dominated Constitutional Convention. The vast chamber of the Hall of Congress was filled with senior members of the armed forces, members of the diplomatic corps, and Perónista Congressmen who overflowed into the opposition benches of the Radical deputies who had refused to attend. As the President took the oath on a bible provided by Evita's foundation, outside a crowd of over 100,000 packed into the three-block Plaza de Congreso echoed his promise to defend the new constitution. At that point, the ceremony turned into a Perónista rally, much to the embarrassment of the diplomats and generals, who were crushed so tight in the hall there was no way they could get out. 'Evita' was chanted over and over again. As she responded with smiles and blown kisses, the crowd whooped into the party marching song, 'The Perónista Boys' —

> We Perónista boys
> Fighting together
> Will ever cry
> With heartfelt joy
> Viva Perón! Viva Perón!

Evita was now more powerful than ever. Through her foundation, her control of radio stations and newspapers, her presence permeated every town and home in Argentina. There was no escape. Her picture dominated the hoardings. Her thoughts were broadcast every few hours throughout the day on nation-wide radio. Her name graced the country's largest gas works and its biggest passenger liner. A newly discovered star was named after her. So was a new downtown Buenos Aires underground station, where the words 'Eva Perón' were bordered with light and her portrait in coloured tile gazed on all passersby.

There was a Maria Eva Duarte de Perón Street in Rosario, an Eva Perón Avenue in Tucuman, an Eva Perón surgical pavilion in San Juan, an Evita City housing project near the federal airport in Buenos Aires, an Evita mainline railway station, and two Evita songs — the 'Eva Perón March' and 'Captain Evita'.

135

Both were sung at the opening ceremony of the Western hemisphere's own Olympics, the first Pan-American Games, which were held in Argentina in February 1951. Athletes and officials from seventeen nations in the hemisphere were given a full dose of Peronism at its most spectacular. Entering the flood-lit, flag-decked arena in a limousine, Evita and her husband were wildly cheered by the huge crowd packed into the new vast soccer bowl built by Evita's foundation in the Avellaneda meat packing district of Buenos Aires. Two of her sayings, in letters six foot high, rimmed the facade of the upper tier. A section of the stadium bearing her name was filled with thousands of children waving Argentine flags with 'Perón' and 'Evita' printed on either side of the flag's white stripe. Throughout the programme a guard of honour of the nurses of the Eva Perón Foundation formed a spectacular aisle of dark blue and white across the grass.

During the ritual of the opening ceremonies — the lighting of the Olympic flame and President Perón's greeting to the hundreds of athletes — Evita dominated the scene in the official tribunal. An Argentine girl athlete presented her with an enormous bunch of flowers on behalf of all the participating women. Her influence was also apparent during the taking of the Olympic oath. Contrary to the Olympic practice until then, both a man and a woman took the collective oath together. Afterwards, Avery Brundage, the president of the Pan-American Games Committee, offered a tribute to Señora Perón, 'without whose enthusiastic support' the games would not have been possible. What he meant was that Evita had paid the bills, or rather her foundation had, which was the same thing. Adulation also came from beyond the borders of Argentina. Bolivia adorned her with the Order of the Condor of the Andes. The Colombians gave her the Cross of Boyaca. She held the Peruvian Grand Cross of the Order of the Sun, Mexico's Order of the Aztec Eagle, and Ecuador's Grand Cross of the Order of Merit for 'the spontaneous and generous manner in which she contributed to the relief of the grief of the victims' of Ecuador's 1949 earthquake.

She was only thirty-one years old, and already countrymen and women of hers were venerating her as a saint. So perhaps it was no wonder there were signs that she was beginning to lose touch with reality. She told the country's provincial governors with a straight face and the utmost sincerity that Argentina's children were now learning to say Perón before they said papa.

She told a reporter that 'at times, in my travels, I have seen in the eyes of children, women and even men an expression of adoration, as though I was a supernatural being. I believe this happens precisely because the difference between living conditions in Argentina in the days of the oligarchy and now is almost as great to simple and humble minds as the difference between the natural and the supernatural. An example that confirms what I am saying is that in Jujuy a child approached me and said, "Mama Eva, give me your benediction."'

But there was no benediction for her enemies, nor a spark of forgiveness for the conspirators she saw behind every lamp-post. General Sosa Molina's obsequiousness during his luncheon for Evita did not save his job. He was kicked upstairs as Minister of Defence. Theoretically, he was still in control of the armed forces but in actual fact he no longer had personal contact with any of them.

Foreign Minister Juan Bramuglia lost his job, too, though no one ever knew just why Evita hated her husband's oldest friend so violently. Perhaps the international praise for his statesmanship — he played a major role in settling the Berlin crisis of 1948 — provoked the Señora's jealousy. But most knowledgeable Argentines felt that it was an old score Evita was settling — that she believed Bramuglia had not moved quickly enough to help Perón when he was temporarily ousted from power in October 1945. There were some who believed it was the other way around — that after Perón's arrest, Evita had pleaded with Bramuglia to help get her out of the country, that he had told her to pull herself together, and he had then roused the meat packers to march into the city and restore Perón to his Casa Rosada balcony.

Such heretical re-writing of one of the classic stories of Peron mythology possessed some credence. Evita's old actress friend, Pierina Dealessi, claimed that Evita had hidden in her house during those tempestuous days. 'She thought they had killed Perón and would probably kill her, too,' recalled Pierina. 'I'll never forget her look of terror when she came to my house.' Whatever the truth, Evita saw to it that Bramuglia's name was never mentioned in the Perónista press, not even when he met US President Harry S. Truman or signed a new Argentine accord with Italy. He had to go, and in the end he did.

Even Miguel Miranda, Perón's economic czar and the man in charge of the country's industrialisation programme, found himself hurriedly packing a bag to catch a boat across the river because he had provoked the wrath of the Señora. They had been business partners. In fact, Miranda was the money man behind Evita's newspaper and radio purchases. But that did not save him. He had made the mistake of confiding to a group of wool exporters that it was not his fault that they were getting such poor prices from the government for their wool. It was Señora Perón who set the price of wool, he told them, as she did everything else in Argentina. As Argentina's farmers hated Miranda, anyway, for bleeding them dry to keep his industrialisation programme going, they had little compunction in passing on the contents of that conversation to the Señora. Twenty-four hours later, Miranda was resting in a hotel room in Montevideo.

Others were not so lucky. Eighteen reporters were sacked and blacklisted by their newspapers after the eagle-eyed Presidenta had spotted their failure to applaud her husband's speech at the State opening of Congress. A young porteño was jailed because he publicly refused to hand over his jack-pot radio quiz show winnings to Evita's foundation. Even suave, handsome Jose Maria de Areilza, Count of Motrico, the Spanish Ambassador to Argentina, found out what it was like to get on the wrong side of the Señora. When negotiations with Spain for a new trade agreement turned out badly for Argentina, he was peremptorily summoned to the Residence, where he was kept twiddling his thumbs in the hall for two hours. Finally, he heard Perón yell to Evita, wanting to know who it was downstairs. 'That *mierda de gallego*,' yelled back Argentina's First Lady. As mierda means shit and gallego is the crude Argentine name for Spaniards based on the assumption that they all come from the province of Galicia, Ambassador de Areilza called a servant over and smilingly asked him to inform the Señora that the gallego had to leave but the mierda would be staying. He caught the next boat back to Spain, and that was the end of the three quarters of a million pounds which Franco had invested in Evita's visit to Madrid.

Evita did not have a sense of humour, as the Count of Motrico obviously knew when he made his parting remark. But then humour is not a national characteristic of the Argentines, perhaps because of their almost painful obsession with *dignidad*, a quality which *New York Times* reporter Milton Bracker once described as a two-way variable, approaching all pride at one extreme and no sense of humour at the other.

Time magazine, after constant blacklisting, found itself on Evita's permanent banned list with a story about the ceremonial return to Argentina of the remains of the parents of General Jose de San Martin, the national hero. The story described the solemnity of the rites and ended by quoting a remark by a youthful onlooker: 'Next year they're going to bring back his horse.' To the Argentines it was a national insult. The Ambassador in Washington protested. Demands were made for the expulsion of the *Time* correspondent in Buenos Aires. Finally, to wipe out the stain, the National San Martin Institute publicly laid a wreath on a monument, not of San Martin, but of George Washington in order to close the incident in a manner best befitting the *dignidad* of Argentina. But *Time*, along with *Newsweek*, *Life*, and other American publications, were seized at the airport whenever they were found in passengers' baggage.

There is no room for a free press in a dictatorship. As Argentina is rarely without the latter, there have been few periods in the country's modern history when it has enjoyed a truly free press.

Through her hand-picked minions in the Ministry of Information, Evita had closed nearly 100 newspapers and magazines by 1951. Most of them had died a 'legal' death. Some were closed because they failed to observe a government decree that obliged all newspapers to carry at the top of each page — 'the year of the Liberator General San Martin'. Others criticising the Peróns — like the small daily *El Intransigente* in the northwestern town of Salta which always called the President 'the nazi colonel' — were strangled by a newsprint squeeze, which the government operated because it controlled all supplies of newsprint. But there were other 'legal' ways. *Los Principios*, an influential catholic daily in Cordoba, was closed because the paint on its walls was not fresh enough and some of its windows had broken panes. Sometimes the reasons were more personal. *Que*, a weekly news magazine, published a cover story on Libertad Lamarque, the actress who once slapped Evita's face. She had fled to Mexico after the Peróns came to power, and her movies were banned in Argentina. So it was somewhat provocative of *Que* to put Libertad's face on its cover. The printers refused to permit the distributors to remove the issue from their plant. It was *Que*'s last magazine. No printer would handle it after that.

But *Que* was a minor matter compared to the Peróns' onslaught on the country's largest and most famous newspaper,

La Prensa of Buenos Aires. From its grey granite building on Avenida de Mayo, *La Prensa* had been a thorn in the side of dictatorial governments in Argentina since its first issue in 1869, although Perón had a different view of that, too. 'For a hundred years,' he thundered, '*La Prensa* has pontificated with endless lies and imbecilities.' The first shots in the battle were fired in 1944 when Perón, then Minister of War, closed the paper for five days for 'distorting the truth and misleading public opinion'. A year later, he briefly jailed *La Prensa*'s owner-editor, Dr Alberto Gainza Paz, along with Dr Luis Mitre, the elderly owner of *La Nacion*, another leading opposition paper.

La Nacion tried to steer a cautious, non-aggressive line after that. Not so *La Prensa*. Consequently, nine months after Perón's inauguration as president, he publicly turned the Perónista mob against the paper. He had four enemies, he shouted from his balcony, the oligarchy, opposition politicians, communists, and *La Prensa*. As far as Evita was concerned, two of those — the oligarchy and the newspaper — were one and the same. In saying this, she was not far wrong. The editorial policy of the wealthy Paz family and the interests of the land-owning aristocracy usually coincided when it came to deciding the national interest. And *La Prensa* had never campaigned against the feudal peonage of the country's peasants or against the appalling low wages and working conditions of city workers! That in itself was enough to doom the paper in Evita's eyes. But there was a personal grudge to settle as well. The Paz family, like other well-to-do Argentines, simply could not stomach the thought of that woman as the nation's First Lady. Her name was banned in the news columns (she was referred to as the president's wife) and no matter how distinguished her guests, her dinners and parties never made the paper's society columns. Her pride was outraged and this was a strong reason for harassing *La Prensa*.

She appealed for a 'patriotic' boycott of the paper. Her Ministry of Information plastered the city with posters reading '*La Prensa* against the country', and the State radio attacked it three times a day for 28 days. But to Evita's dismay, she found out that as much as she attacked it so its circulation increased. She embarked on tougher measures. The paper was told that long lines of would-be advertisers blocked traffic. Two boilers in its rotogravure plant were condemned and the paper was forced to close down while they were replaced. A new customs duty, back-dated twelve years, was levied on its imported newsprint. Citing a national shortage, the government removed thousands of tons of newsprint already in the paper's warehouse. For the same reason it ordered a cut in the number of pages each day, first to 16 pages, then to 12. Armed federal police raided the newspaper's editorial offices after it published a story on the torture of political prisoners. Perón sued it for libel. Evita decreed restrictions on classified advertising, the paper's lifeblood. Houses could only be advertised on certain days. On others, only job seekers could buy space. Government employment advertisements had to be run free. And to further intimidate *La Prensa* readers, people who wanted to place advertisements in the paper had to get government permission, which meant that their names would go down on police files as being anti-Perónista. But Gainza Paz still refused to stop his attacks on the government, and the paper's circulation continued to soar from a pre-war 250,000 to over half a million. When Evita cut its newsprint supply yet again, porteños passed each day's copy from hand to hand. In the end, thanks to Evita's war on it, *La Prensa*, for all its faults, had become a symbol of embattled freedom, a rallying point for the government's enemies. It had to die.

The fatal blow fell during the course of a railway strike early in 1951, the government's second major conflict with the unions in two years. Evita had settled that earlier newspaper strike by importing printers from the provinces, and many of those strikers permanently lost their jobs. But the railway workers were a tougher breed. Defying CGT orders, 180,000 of them launched a series of strikes that threatened to cripple the economy of the country. Evita talked and pleaded with them. Orlando Martinez, a retired railway worker, remembers Evita climbing aboard a handcart with him to pump their way along the tracks five miles outside Buenos Aires to convince railway workers to abandon the strike.

'When we got there,' he recalled, 'she stood up perspiring heavily and said that Perón had sent her to ask them to return to their jobs. They cheered her wildly and the strike was broken. The two or three bolsheviks were left there standing alone.' That's how Perónistas fondly remember those days. But it was not quite like that.

The strike did not end right there and then. But the trains did stop running, and on the walls in poorer parts of Buenos Aires, normally solid Perónista territory, scrawled signs said ominously '*Viva Perón Viudo!* (Long Live the Widower Perón).' Evita's newspapers angrily blamed the strike on communists.

141

But strikers on the picket lines shouted: 'We're not communists. We're hungry Perónists.'

Not only was that true, but *La Prensa* discovered that the strike had been triggered by a serious conflict between followers of Evita, on the one hand, and her husband on the other. That was dangerous news. But the paper decided to go ahead and print it. However, that issue of January 26, 1951, never reached the streets of Buenos Aires. Acting on Evita's instructions, the news vendors' union, a CGT affiliate, struck the newspaper that night. The vendors, who were not employees of the paper but independent businessmen, presented Gainza Paz with impossible demands — 20 per cent of the paper's classified advertising income, the abolition of home subscriptions, and the turning over to the vendors of the entire press run of each issue. That, of course, would have placed *La Prensa* firmly under Evita's control. But the publisher refused to knuckle under. Nor would his workers, though most of them were union members themselves. Thirteen hundred of them — editors, reporters, printers, machine-room men, drivers, and clerks — issued a statement saying that they had no quarrel with their boss and they wanted to go back to work. 'This adhesion to the paper is determined fundamentally by the ideals of liberty and democracy which inspire the orientation of *La Prensa* . . . We have no conflict with the paper.'

By the end of February it was obvious to *La Prensa*'s workers that Evita was not going to allow the strike to end. So they tried to march back to work through the picket line set up by the CGT. The pickets opened fire, killing a printer and wounding 14 other *La Prensa* employees. Two months later, Congress expropriated the paper and handed it over to the CGT. A neon-lighted placard went up over the main entrance, proclaiming '*Ahora es Argentina*! (Now it is Argentine!)' On top of the building, *La Prensa*'s famous torch of freedom was covered by giant tinted portraits of Perón and Evita. From his balcony at the Casa Rosada, Perón told crowds still as large as ever in the plaza below that: 'This newspaper, which for so many years exploited the workers and the poor, which was a refined instrument serving national and international exploiters in the crudest treason to our country — this newspaper shall make up for its crimes by serving the workers and defending their gains and rights.' The 'arch-criminal', Alberto Gainza Paz, fled across the river to Uruguay just one step ahead of the federal police. All newspapers in the United States, Canada, and Latin America (except in Argentina) flew flags at half-mast in mourning for *La Prensa*. Evita, with the opposition securely muzzled now, moved ahead with her plans to become Vice-President of Argentina.

12

'MY LIFE FOR PERON'

Two one-legged men, one minus his right leg, the other his left, rode bicycles from Sunday to Friday. Another man drove his car around his neighbourhood for 123 hours and 10 minutes without stopping. A chauffeur from the Ministry of Education topped that by driving continuously for 129 hours and five minutes. A third motorist made a shorter run — backwards. Mario Aldo Tordo and his wife, Delia, carried their baby daughter, Maria, on foot over one-fourth the length of Argentina. He wore a sweat shirt inscribed 'Perón Keeps His Promises'; the front of her shirt read, 'Evita Dignifies'. One man walked across the pampas with a bag of wheat on his shoulder. And Juan Martin, a municipal employee from the town of Santa Fé walked atop a rolling barrel from the city of Rosario to Buenos Aires — a distance of 222 miles. All of them had one thing in mind — they wanted to publicise their wish that Evita should become Vice-President of Argentina.

The date of the election had been brought forward from February, 1952, to November 11, 1951. The months were rolling by and still the Señora had not publicly announced her willingness to accept the honor her descamisados wanted to confer on her. Troubles with the railwaymen — several hundred were goaled and a number tortured before that strike came to end — did not seem to have diminished her popularity. And her schedule was as killing as ever. During one three-day period, she drove to Rosasio, 190 miles from the capital, made three speeches, opened a railway workers' housing project, and drove home; the next morning she flew to San Juan, 750 miles away, to attend the funeral of the Governor. On the third day she was up at 5.30 as usual, held an audience at the residence at 8 o'clock, was in her office by 11 o'clock, attended a meeting of brewery workers in the afternoon and a meeting of railway workers in the evening. Then at 11 o'clock that same night she set off on a five-day trip deep into the interior — attending the inauguration of the Governor of Tucuman, opening a new school and a children's clinic in Jujuy, another school in Catamarca, and distributing gifts to children in a park in Cordoba.

She was on the move so much that she said her husband had begun to scold her for keeping such impossible hours. One of the reasons for this was that she preferred to drive home from long trips with her bodyguards rather than fly, often getting back to the residence in the small hours of the morning. Then she usually invited the lads in for a drink (she drank little herself and did not smoke although she had her own carmine-tipped cigarettes) and they would talk politics until an angry President yelled down the stairs at them: Get rid of those damned *atorrantes* (bums)!' At that point Evita would shoo them out of the front door with a '*Raja muchachos* (hurry up boys), the old man's getting mad'.

Such was the pace of her life that her blonde beauty had taken on a glacial withdrawn quality, giving her face more and more the appearance of a mask. Fleur Cowles, when she saw her, thought she had a strained, tired look — 'the greenness of her skin could only be some sort of warning. I thought she must have had a touch of jaundice ... the gossip in Paris by Argentine friends was that she was dangerously ill with leukaemia.' If so, she gave no hint of it in the fierce pace of her life. When a US Assistant Secretary of State visited Argentina, Evita almost caused him to have a heart attack as she raced him up and down seven flights of stairs to show him every last room in a new 600 bed hospital built by her foundation.

She also found time to march into the Casa Rosada at the head of a small army of her Perónista Woman's Party to present her husband with a gold watch and a demand that he run for President again. He thanked her, but did not say anything about the Vice-Presidency. After all, the country already had a Vice-President, 74-year-old Hortensio Jazmin Quijano, although he was a sick man and in hospital. He did not want to run again,

146

and there was some talk among a few top Perónista officials that Perón's old friend and army colleague, Colonel Domingo Mercante, the Governor of Buenos Aires Province, should get the nod. But Evita's loyal allies in the CGT had different ideas. They announced plans for a monster rally to be held on August 22 in the 450-foot wide Avenida Nueve de Julio and they promised that two million Argentines would be there to proclaim Juan Perón and Evita Perón as their candidates for the nation's two top jobs.

Since Perón assumed the Presidency in 1946, the weather had always been fine for his national fiestas. He had his usual good luck again this time, even though August is very much a winter month in Buenos Aires. The skies were clear as the descamisados began to pour into the city by train, river steamer, lorry, bicycle, and three Model-T Fords which chugged 2,500 kilometres from Patagonia. The country people could easily be spotted on the streets with their black hats, tanned skins and ponchos. Everything was free for them — transport, food, and lodging. Thousands slept overnight in the city garages, requisitioned by the government. Free films and sporting events were laid on to entertain them. The CGT declared a general strike so that everybody could attend. As a result, the normal life of the city was virtually paralysed. But the crowds were orderly and good natured, and the government had wisely removed a possible source of disorder by cancelling three football games (football in Argentina is a sport that has been known to turn into near war on occasions).

As the throngs streamed into the vast avenida they chanted their battle-cry: 'Viva Perón!' 'Viva Evita!' and 'Perón fulfills his promises!' Loudspeaker vans edged through the crowds playing 'We are the Perónist Boys', and 'Evita our Captain'. Huge portraits of the Peróns and election slogans hung from government buildings. The noise of the chanting and the songs boomed out from the loudspeakers attached to every lamp-post on the avenida. It sounded as if every Argentine in the country was there that afternoon. But in fact only 250,000 of them greeted President Perón as he stepped up on to the flood-lit platform, decorated with blue and white Argentine flags.

Evita was not with him, and that brought immediate cries of 'Where is she?' It was the cue for Jose Espejo to speak up: 'My General,' he said: 'we note one absence, the absence of your wife, of Eva Perón, she who is without peer in the world, in history, in the love and veneration of the Argentine people.

147

Companions, possibly her modesty, which is perhaps the greatest of her merits, has kept her from this gathering, but we cannot continue without Comrade Eva Perón.' So an escort of CGT officials was dispatched to the Residence to fetch her. Fifteen minutes later she was there on the platform, hatless, in an elegant suit, raising her arms in acknowledgement of the roar of the crowd.

After the national anthem had been played, Espejo asked the President to stand for re-election. His acceptance was unqualified. But when the CGT leader turned to his boss and called on her to accept the nomination for the Vice-Presidency, she hesitated. First she attacked her old enemies, the oligarchs. They could not attack General Perón directly because of the people's support for him, she said. But they felt they could attack him through her. She was willing, she cried, for her breast to shield her General from all attack. But as for the Vice-Presidency, she asked for four days to make up her mind. From the vast crowd, which seemed to stretch endlessly down the avenida, came the cry that no one would leave until she said yes. She pleaded for twenty-four hours, then two hours. The crowd roared 'now, now.' In a half whisper, she promised: 'I will do what the people say.'

But something was wrong. Everybody knew that. Official acceptance of the nominations had been set for August 24. But the notification was postponed indefinitely. Rumours of an impending military coupe swept the country. Then on August 30, a Brazilian newspaper, *O Mundo*, owned by a close friend and admirer of the Peróns, Dr Gerald Rocha, carried a story that President Perón had told a group of visiting Brazilian newsmen that his wife could not run for Vice-President because she was too young. If she was 29 years old as she said she was, then she was barred from the Vice-Presidency because one of the qualifications for that office was an age of at least 30. But of course she was not 29. She was born on May 7, 1919, which would have made her 32. Presumably some old-fashioned feminine whim had prompted her to send someone to Los Toldos after her marriage to tear out the entry of her birth from the registrar's book in the town hall. But no one accepted Perón's excuse about his wife's age, anyway. There continued to be no official word. Perónista Party officials flocked into Buenos Aires. The Superior Council of the Party huddled in secret meetings throughout most of August 31. That evening, Evita put an end to the suspense. She broadcast to the nation.

In a voice that trembled with emotion and sounded hoarse and strained, she said: 'It is my irrevocable decision to refuse the honour which the workers and the people of my country wished to confer on me at the open forum of the 22nd. I declare that this decision was born in my innermost consciousness and is therefore perfectly free and has all the force of my final will.' Her voice broke and there were moments of silence as she seemed to be gathering her strength to continue. 'I have passed the best years of my life at the side of General Perón, my master,' she went on, 'I have no higher goal in life than to continue to serve him and the people of Argentina.' She was not going to retire from public life, she made that quite clear. 'I am not resigning my work, just the honours,' she said, adding that she would continue as a 'humble collaborator of Perón'. Then in a final emotion-charged passage she said: I only want history to say of me: There was a woman alongside General Perón; a woman who took to him the hopes and needs of the people, and her name was Evita.'

It was the army which had forced Evita into retreat. Its sense of *dignidad* had been severely dented during the Perón years of power, humiliations that were angrily blamed on 'petticoat dictatorship' over drinks in the Officers' Club at Campo de Mayo. So the generals told Perón, their old comrade in arms, that they would not accept his wife as Vice-President. The thought of her as their Commander-in-Chief, which she would be if anything happened to him, was too intolerable to contemplate. This time, the generals warned Perón, they would try their hand at revolution if Evita accepted the Perónista nomination, which they knew was tantamount to election. Perhaps the fact that only 250,000 supporters had turned out on August 22, instead of the promised two million, encouraged them to test their strength. Yet by democratic standards it was a remarkable feat to get that number of people together from all over the country — if one forgot that every agency of the government had been geared to the task. Perón complained bitterly that his descamisados had let him down. He might have called the generals' bluff with two million chips, but not with only a quarter-of-a million. It meant that Evita had to step down. But that still did not stop the army from trying to bring about a revolution in any case.

First suspicions were aroused before dawn on September 28, when there was unusual activity around the air base at El

Palomar, about twelve miles west of Buenos Aires. Officers at the military school, which shares El Palomar with the airmen, reported promptly to the President, who, as usual, was at his desk in the Casa Rosada by 6.30 am. He called in his military leaders, but planes were already flying over the capital, dropping leaflets that urged the people to support the revolt against Perón. They carried the name of a retired general, Benjamin Menendez. But other than sweeping so low over the Casa Rosada that they nearly knocked over the chimney pots, the planes did no damage.

Immediately Perón ordered the summary shooting of any uniformed man taking part in the revolt. A state of siege was declared and censorship imposed. Federal police set up guards over radio stations, newspapers, and state banks. Business establishments dropped their heavy steel shutters. The CGT called a general strike and ordered its members into the streets to help defeat the rebels. But there was little to do, except for occasional fist fights in the streets. Police rescued one man from a mob which was chasing him, and loyal troops went into action at El Palomar and Campo de Mayo. The rebels had apparently controlled both bases for a few hours, but by the afternoon the government had won them back. Artillery shells were fired at El Palomar, but they landed on the runway and did no damage. Only one soldier died, a Sergeant Farina who, according to Perónista newspapers, had fallen with the cry of 'Viva Perón' on his lips.

In the afternoon, Perón appeared on his balcony and looked down on a plaza packed with loyal descamisados. 'A group of bad Argentines dishonoured the uniform of the fatherland,' he told them. Contemptuously, he added that the rebels 'at the first shots, raised the white flag and surrendered. They are cowards because they did not dare to die the one time they should have sacrificed life for the sake of their honour,' he said. 'That is why they will suffer the opprobrious penalty of a coward. As cowards, they will be executed,' he promised the cheering supporters. 'Hang them!' Hang them!' shouted the crowd. 'That I will do,' General Perón yelled, banging his fist on the velvet rail of the balcony. 'As an example. Everyone must know that those who in future go out to fight against us either will kill us or we will kill them.' But he did not. Most of the rebels flew off to Uruguay, while General Menendez was thrown in gaol. Juan Perón had more on his mind just then than incompetent revolutionaries. His wife was dying.

She had been taken ill immediately after her renunciation of the Vice-Presidency, suffering from influenza and anaemia, it was said. She had been under treatment for over a year by a Polish blood specialist, Dr Helen Zawarski. Her blood count had fallen to three-fifths of normal. But she had continued her exhausting schedule right up to the moment of her collapse, refusing to pander to the tiredness that must have been tearing at every muscle and bone in her body. When she finally took to her bed, her husband, in tears, told friends that she had pernicious anaemia, which was probably gentle shorthand for leukaemia. However, the news of the attempted coup had her struggling to get out of bed, though in the end she was persuaded to broadcast from there. In a voice that was hardly audible, she expressed her thanks to her descamisados for their support of her husband. 'To all of you I give a great embrace from my heart,' she whispered. 'For me there is nothing in the world but the love of Perón and my people.'

There was still a little strength left. On October 17, a slight figure in a crimson coat appeared on the balcony of the Casa Rosada. She looked frail and haggard. But she managed a smile and a wave for the cheering crowd below. The plaza was packed with her descamisados, just as it had been on October 17 six years earlier. Few of them had known she even existed then. Now they were there to pay her homage. In the new era of television the cameras zoomed in on the tired face as the President pinned on her breast the Grand Peronista Medal, Extraordinary Class, in recognition of her selflessness in renouncing her candidacy. He embraced her and she wept in his arms.

'This marvellous people,' said Perón, turning to the microphones, 'whom we have already qualified as being the best in the world, has decided that this October 17 should be dedicated to Eva Perón. There could be no homage more just, more deep, more honourable than this dedication. She is not only the guide and the standard bearer of our movement but in Argentine history the figure of Eva Perón will be seen as one of the greatest women of humanity.' Then he pleaded for silence so that his wife could speak without strain. As she did so, his hands cradled her waist to prevent her from falling. In the stillness, she began:

'My beloved descamisados, this is a day of great emotion for me. With all my soul I have desired to be with you and with Perón on this glorious day of the descamisados. I could never

151

miss this appointment that I have with the people on each October 17th. I assure you that nothing and no one could have prevented me from coming because I have a sacred debt to Perón and to you, to the workers and the boys of the CGT, and it does not matter to me if in paying it I must leave shreds of my life by the wayside. I had to come and I came to thank Perón and the CGT and the descamisados and my people. To Perón, who has just honoured me with the highest distinction that can be given a Perónista, I shall never finish paying my debt, not until I give my life in gratitude for the kindness he has always shown me. Nothing that I have, nothing that I am, nothing that I think is mine; it is Perón's. I will not tell the usual lie and say that I have not deserved this; yes I deserve it, my General. I deserve it for one thing only that is worth all the gold in the world. I deserve it because all I have done is for love of this country. What I have done is of no value; my renunciation is of no value; what I am and what I have is of no value. I have only one thing of value and that is my heart. It burns in my soul, aches in my flesh, stings in my nerves; it is love for the people and Perón. And I give thanks to you, my General, who have taught me to know you and love you. If the people ask for my life I would give it singing because the happiness of one descamisado is worth more than my life.

'I had to come to give thanks to the CGT for the laurels with which they have decorated me which are for me the dearest memento of the Argentine workers. I had to come to thank the workers and the CGT who dedicated this day to a humble woman. I had to come to tell you, as I told the General, that it is necessary to keep an alert watch on all sides in our struggle. The danger is not past. The enemies of the people, of Perón and of the patria do not sleep. It is necessary that each Argentine worker keeps on the lookout and that he should not sleep, for the enemies work in the shadow of treason and sometimes they hide behind a smile or an outstretched hand. I had to come to thank all my beloved descamisados from every corner of the patria because on September 28 you knew how to risk your lives for Perón. I was sure you would know, as you have known before, how to act as a trench for Perón. The enemies of Perón and of the patria have known for a long time that Perón and Eva Perón are ready to die for the people. Now they know that the people are ready to die for Perón. I just ask one thing of you today, comrades, that we all swear publicly to defend Perón and to fight for him and we will shout our oath aloud for the space of one minute so that the sound of it may reach the furthest corners of the world.'

The roar of 'My life for Perón' echoed and re-echoed round the plaza. Then she continued.

'I thank you, comrades, for your prayers for my health. I thank you from my heart. I hope that God hears the humble people of my patria so that I may soon return to the battle and continue fighting with Perón for you and with you for Perón until death. I have wanted and I want nothing for myself. My glory is and always will be the shield of Perón and the banner of my people, and even if I leave shreds of my life on the wayside I know that you will gather them up in my name and carry them like a flag to victory. I know that God is with us because he is with the humble and despises the pride of the oligarchs, and so the victory will be ours. Sooner or later we will reach it, cost what it may and fall who must.

'My descamisados, I would like to say many things to you but the doctors have told me I must not talk. I leave you my heart and I tell you I am sure, as it is my wish, that I shall soon be in the fight again, with more strength and more love, to fight for this country that I love so much, as I love Perón. I ask only one thing of you: I am sure that I will soon be with you, but if because of my health I cannot, help Perón, be loyal to Perón as you have been until now, because this is to be loyal to the patria and to yourselves. And all those descamisados of the interior, I embrace them very close to my heart and I hope that they realise how much I love them.'

The passion, the love, the hatred, it was all there as before. But there was a difference. The crowd knew it. There were many men as well as women weeping openly in the plaza. On November 6, she was operated on for cancer of the uterus. Her newspaper, *Democracia*, said that before she went under the anaesthetic she cried, 'Viva Perón!' which must have shaken Dr George T. Pack, the New York Memorial Hospital cancer specialist who performed the operation.

Five days later a special ballot box was carried to her bedside so that she could vote in the presidential election. She had broadcast to the nation the night before and, weak though she was, there was nothing soft in her words. 'Not to vote for Perón,' she said, 'is for an Argentine — I say it because I feel it — to betray the country.' She warned the voters that she would be with them in spirit. 'I will follow you like a shadow, repeating in your ears and your conscience the name of Perón until you have

153

deposited your vote in the urn as a message of love and of faith and of loyalty towards the leader of the people. May every Perónista vote on November 11 be a silent cry from an Argentine heart, "My life for Perón!"

For her vote to be legal there had to be a poll watcher of an opposition party present. David Vinas, an Argentine novelist, never forgot that moment. He was a member of the Radical Party. 'It was a rainy day and we three went in — a member of the election board carrying the ballot box, a Perónista party representative, and me. For a moment we were in the hospital room alone with her. Awed. Her face was made up but quite drawn. Her legs were bent and spread out. On her hospital bed were the different ballots of all the parties. We had to leave her alone to vote and when we came back they were all there but the Perónist ballot. But the most impressive moment of all came when we left and walked through the women kneeling in the entrance and outside the hospital. They were kneeling in the rain and reaching up to try and touch the ballot box because Evita had touched it and her vote was inside. A ballot box had acquired mystical properties!'

There was nothing mystical about the result of the election. There would have been if the opposition Radical Party had won. Its candidates were allowed no newspaper space or radio time and had to depend on rallies to get their message across. But even the rallies were restricted in number and harried by the police. The polling itself was scrupulously honest, as it had been in 1946. The army made sure of that. Even so, Perón piled up an impressive sixty-six per cent of the vote. His party won all 30 Senate seats and all but 14 of 149 places in the Chamber of Deputies. Perónista Governors were elected in all 14 provinces. In some areas of the interior Perón amassed a five to one margin over his opponents. But it was Evita's Perónista Woman's Party that performed the best of all. Most of the four million Argentine women voting for the first time cast their ballot for Perón. Not only that, they elected six women Senators and 23 women Deputies. Women were also elected to provincial legislatures, and to municipal, town, and village offices. The old Hispanic attitude of male superiority was never going to have the same force again in Argentina, although the woman who had made that possible had been stopped from holding office herself.

Ironically, she sat in the Vice-President's traditional place when Juan Perón took the oath of office on June 4, 1952, to

154

succeed himself as President of Argentina for another six-year term. She sat there because the place was vacant; Vice-President Hortensio Quijano had died since the November election. She looked desperately ill herself, clad in an ankle length mink coat that covered her shrunken body like a shroud. At the Congress building, Perón guided her faltering steps to the Vice-President's chair, then quickly, with one hand on the bible, swore to defend the constitution. Outside, thousands of members of the Perónista Woman's Party chanted: 'Viva Evita, the Vice-President'. But Evita slipped away to return to the presidential estate in suburban Olivos. Perón swore in his new Cabinet, reviewed a parade of cavalry and foot soldiers, waved briefly to 100,000 descamisados in the plaza, and hurried to Olivos to be at his wife's side.

13

DEATH OF THE LEGEND

That was the last time the descamisados saw their beloved Evita. She was dying. The cancer she had fought off for so long was spreading swiftly with agonising pain through her body. But the Argentine people did not know, although they began to suspect she was more than merely ill when neither she nor her husband put in an appearance at the traditional Flag Day ceremonies on June 19. When she failed to appear at the Independence Day parade on July 9, her doctors tried to still the rumours with a bulletin stating that she needed rest. But, by then, word had leaked out from the Olivos mansion that she was being fed intravenously.

At the Avenida de Mayo headquarters of the Sub-Secretary of Information, lights burned all night as a special watch of five reporters waited for news of Evita's health. Perónist leaders, hearing through the political grapevine that death was only a matter of days away, scrambled to outdo each other in their tributes. The Governor of Buenos Aires Province, Carlos Aloe, ordered Evita's autobiography to be used as a reader in the first grade of Argentine schools, as a textbook for civics courses in the fifth and sixth grades, and in translation as the supplementary text in language courses. Health Minister Ramon Carillo directed that in 508 hospitals and clinics under his department masses should be said for her 'quick and complete recovery'.

In the Congress, the Perónist majority voted to build a huge marble and bronze monument to her, with 24 replicas for each of Argentina's provinces and territories. During one of the 59 impassioned speeches that were made in praise of Evita, Perónista Deputy Mafalda Piovano dropped on her knees in the aisle and prayed: 'Oh God, we beseech you to return to Eva Perón the health she has sacrificed to save us.' Then the Congresswoman fainted dead away. As soon as she was revived, President of the Chamber Hector J. Campora led the 124 Perónista deputies in swearing loyalty to Perón as President and to Evita as 'Spiritual Chief of the Nation' — the title by which she had been formally listed in Argentina's Congressional Record since her final public appearance at her husband's inaugural.

The entire Argentine nation was also given its part to play in the homage. Given a half-day holiday, vast crowds stood silently for ten minutes in dusty plazas in cities, towns and villages across the country to demonstrate their love for their dying First Lady. But, as always where Eva Perón was concerned, anger and hatred were as visible as love on that blustery winter's afternoon.

In Luna Park Stadium, Evita's old friend, Jose Espejo, the CGT General-Secretary, whipped a crowd of 50,000 Peronistas into a frenzy with a virulent attack on the American Government, which, he claimed, had prevented the words of their saint from reaching the workers of America. The State Department, he said, had conspired with US publishers to stop an English language version of Evita's autobiography from being printed in the United States. A backdrop of posters showed a pink octopus sitting on a heap of skulls and gold coins holding Wall Street in one hand and a hatchet in the other directed at Eva Perón's book. Another showed a voracious-looking black eagle wearing stars and stripes on its neckband swooping down on the same volume. Screamed Espejo: 'Those clippers of coupons in Wall Street, the Vatican of the dollar, are silencing the voice of love and justice. The hungry wolves of Yankee Imperialism are terrified that our fellow American workers will learn about Argentina's happiness and abundance.' But the labour leader promised his delighted audience that the CGT would be sending a copy of Evita's book to every worker in the United States.

That never happened of course. If it had, the reaction of American workers would certainly have been the same as that of a growing number of Argentines. For in the few cities captured by the Radical Party in the November Presidential elections, Radical Mayors removed portraits of Eva Perón, as well as copies of her book, from their city halls and burnt them. The Mayors claimed that as she held no official government post, her picture and autobiography had no right to be cluttering up their offices. It was a brave thing to do in a nation where the cult of Evita had reached a pitch of hysteria. But it was not very wise.

In the two largest cities where it happened, Juarez, 230 miles south of Buenos Aires with a population of 54,000, and Salta, with 25,000 inhabitants, 110 miles northwest of the capital, Perónista workers paralysed both municipalities with general strikes in protest against the mayors' actions. That gave the fanatical governor of Buenos Aires Province, Carlos Aloe, the opportunity, which he quickly took, to throw out the Radical Mayors and replace them with Perónista Mayors on the grounds that city government had broken down, endangering the welfare of the citizens. There was not even a pretence at making a legalistic examination of the rights and wrongs of the situation. For by mid-winter of 1952, Perónismo had become the law in Argentina, and there was no more fervent upholder of the new judicial order than Carlos Aloe, who had changed the oath of office when he became Governor to include the statement that he was ruling the province on behalf of Juan and Eva Perón.

Such obsequiousness would have earned warm public praise from the Peróns in earlier days. But at Olivos there was no thought for anything but the approach of death. The weekly Cabinet meetings were cancelled. The President was spending most of his waking hours by his wife's bedside, holding her hand as she slept, lulled by powerful pain-killing drugs. During one of her periods of consciousness, he presented her with the Collar of the Order of San Martin, named after the nineteenth-century general who led Argentina's war of liberation against the Spanish. Of all the millions of pounds worth of jewellery that Eva Perón acquired with such squirrel-like zeal during her brief years of power, this gleaming decoration topped them all. The collar contained 758 diamonds, emeralds and rubies, bridged by 3,800 gold and platinum elements. The main pendant consisted of a diamond and emerald rosette, containing an image of Argentina's liberator against a background of 16 rays of gold and platinum. No matter that the Collar of San Martin is specifically reserved in Argentine law as an honour for chiefs of state. As Eva's tired, glazed eyes stared at the sparkling Collar lying on her lap on top of her blankets and her bone-thin fingers rubbed over the jewels, she knew only too well the terrible, ironic reason for the award. It meant that when she died she would be eligible for presidential burial.

Outside the walled grounds of the residence, Perónista women kneeled sobbing on the pavement at all hours of the day and night. Apparently, the sound of the crying must have penetrated the silent, shuttered house. For on July 16, Federal police moved the growing crowds back across the street and posted notices around the neighbourhood calling for 'no noise'. Two days later, all traffic was diverted from the area and even Cabinet Ministers had to walk the final few hundred yards to the gate of the residence. On the Sunday, July 21, thousands of porteños assembled in heavy rain for an open air mass in the centre of Buenos Aires, where Evita's priest, Father Benitez, who had accompanied her famous trip around Europe, petitioned for 'the miracle of her restoration'. In a last despairing bid for human help, President Perón called in two German cancer experts, Professor Paul Uhlenbruck of Cologne, a heart and blood circulation specialist, and Professor Heinrich Kalk of Kassel, a liver specialist. They arrived on July 24 and were rushed straight from their plane to Olivos, police outriders clearing the way for their car. But it was too late.

On the afternoon of July 26, Evita's doctors reported that their 'illustrious patient' had declined markedly. Sometime during that afternoon, according to her own newspaper, *Democracia*, the pain-racked woman whispered to her husband: 'If I have committed any sins in life I am paying sufficiently for them by this pain. I kissed many tubercular workers thinking God would not send me pain because I did it for the poor. Now God sends me this. It is too much but if it is His work it is well.'

She was sinking fast. A second bulletin at 6.10 pm reported her condition as serious. At 7 o'clock it was announced that she had lapsed into unconsciousness fifteen minutes earlier. At 8.25, the crowds keeping a hushed but tearful vigil across the street from the residence saw a dim light snapped out in a second floor room. Inside the darkened chamber, President Perón walked away from the bedside of his wife. To waiting family and Cabinet Ministers he said, simply: 'Evita is dead.' At her death, the once beautiful woman weighed a gaunt 80 pounds. On that cold July night, for the second time in his life, Juan Perón was looking down at a wife dead of cancer.

All through the night Argentine radio stations interrupted

their programmes of religious music with the news that 'the Sub-Secretariat of Information fulfills the very sad duty of announcing that at 8.25 o'clock Señora Eva Perón, the spiritual leader of the nation, passed away.' Churches throughout the country tolled a slow, mournful death-knell. The Cabinet met to declare all official activities suspended for two days, with 30 days of official mourning. Outside the Olivos residence, a man with a crepe-draped Argentine flag perched himself in the fork of a tree and announced dramatically that he would stay there for ever. (Rain soon forced him down.)

Inside the house, Dr Pedro Ara, a distinguished Spanish pathologist who was cultural attaché at the Spanish Embassy in Buenos Aires, was taken by President Perón to Evita's bedroom to prepare the body for the next day's lying in state at the Ministry of Labour. 'Her face,' recalled Ara, 'had a tranquil, beautiful look, liberated at last from her cruel suffering. * One of her doctors, Dr Ricardo Finochietto, had closed her eyes and placed her face in repose. Her mother and her priest, Father Benitez, knelt praying by the bed. 'I'm going to give you all the keys to my poor wife's room,' Peron told him. 'No one will be able to enter — not the family nor myself — while you are working.'

Through the windows of Eva Perón's room, looking out over the grounds to the River Plate, Dr Ara could see the first light of dawn piercing through the storm clouds as he finished his initial work on the body. There were still many more months of work to be done to complete the embalming process. But as he had told Perón the previous night, the success or failure of the embalming process depended critically on those first few hours. But Ara was satisfied now that the body was incorruptible. There was a knock on the door. It was Evita's dressmaker and hairdresser. Like Ara, the dressmaker had worked through the night cutting and sewing her mistress's final robe. 'She looks as though she is sleeping,' she said as she dressed her. Evita's hairdresser, Julio, who had known since she was a little girl in Junin, told Ara that during her years in government he had always had the honour of being her first visitor in the morning. 'No one else cut her hair. I even went to Spain with her,' he said proudly. 'If I could just . . .' Ara cut him short. 'Go ahead, maestro,' he told Julio. 'Perform your art for the last time. But be quick. They are waiting.' It took the hairdresser an hour to

* From his book, *El Caso de Eva Peron.*

161

comb and arrange Evita's hair, during which time her brother, Juan Duarte, came in and cut off a long silver lock to take to their mother.

Just as Ara was placing her hands around the rosary of silver and mother of pearl that had been given to her by the Pope, one of her maids walked in with her manicurist kit. 'Doctor,' she said, 'before her final moments of suffering, the Señora told me: 'When I die, take off the red varnish and replace it with a plain varnish.'' The astonished doctor was speechless. He could not believe that the dying woman could have been thinking about such things, consumed as she was with such pain. But just at the moment Perón entered the room. 'It's true,' he said, 'I heard her. Go ahead and do it, Señorita.' Then Perón turned to Ara. 'Tell me doctor. How long will the body remain like this before it decomposes?' The doctor, who often carried in his luggage the head of an old peasant that he had embalmed, much to the consternation of customs officers in various parts of the world, said quite firmly: 'General, it will never decompose.'

Perón then told him that after the Argentine people had been given a few days to see the body, he would have as long as he wanted to finish the embalming process at CGT headquarters, where it was to be kept until the giant monument and crypt that Perón had planned for her in the centre of Buenos Aires was ready. Ara demurred. He pointed out as diplomatically as he could that the CGT was not the quietest place or the most peaceful for doing the kind of delicate work that he had in front of him. There had even been occasions when the place had become the target of disturbances and fights. But Perón just shook his head as Ara suggested that he would much rather do his work in a hospital or even in the grounds of the Olivos residence. 'No, professor,' he said. 'My wife asked that her mortal remains be placed in the CGT until they could be moved to the crypt in the monument, and I'm going to do exactly what she wanted. But I can assure you that you will have all the peace and security that you need. Part of the building is being turned into a laboratory for you. And the men who looked after my wife while she was alive are from today under your orders. Everybody will help you. All the workers adored my wife. To them she was more than a mother.'

There was nothing more to be said. An hour later, a black van slipped out through the main gates of the residence past the unsuspecting mourning throngs. It carried Evita's silver-trimmed, white mahogany coffin to the Ministry of Labour

162

building, where her body was laid in state in the gold-domed room where for six years she had wielded the power that formed the backbone of her husband's regime. The coffin, topped with a full-length glass cover, was placed on a huge horseshoe bier of mauve and white orchids. Flowers covered the second floor auditorium and overflowed into the street. Inevitably, despite the secrecy of the move to enable Perón to pray in peace besides the body and attend a mass conducted by Father Benitez, the word spread swiftly through the city that Evita was at the Ministry. All night vast crowds had kept vigil in the streets, kneeling in prayer on rain-swept pavements. Women wept openly, some in a state of near collapse. Now they swarmed around the Ministry, shouting 'we want to see her'. The police managed to hold them off for a few hours in the morning. But finally the crowds broke through the police line and were only held in check by a second emergency squad at the doors. Then the order was given to admit the people.

The whole nation seemed crazed with grief. All flags were at half-mast and draped in black as were lamp-posts and buildings in every city, town and village. For three days no business of any kind was carried out in Argentina. Buenos Aires, one of the world's great cities, closed down completely. No shops or restaurants were open. There were no buses or taxis. Guests in the elegant Plaza Hotel made their own beds and had to make do on one meal a day. Only the florists remained open and they did a thriving business. Flowers covered the streets around the Ministry of Labour and piled 20 feet high up the walls of the building. When the country's florists were emptied, flowers were flown in from as far away as Chile.

Outside the Ministry, the crowds grew longer and longer. Within a fortnight over two million Argentines had made the pilgrimage to Evita's bier, lining up for more than 15 hours in freezing rain to get a 20-second glimpse of her thin and wasted face. Hysterical women flung themselves forward to kiss the glass of her coffin. Sixteen people were crushed to death by the throngs; over 4,000 were taken to city hospitals to be treated for injuries, and thousands more were give first aid on the spot. To feed the 20-block long, four-a-breast queues, the army set up field kitchens, dispensing free sandwiches and coffee.

Away from the bier, Perónista groups around the country unremittingly tried to outdo each other in paying homage to their First Lady. The eloquence of the oratory was typified by a senator in the Congress who claimed that Evita had not only combined the best virtues of Catherine the Great of Russia, Queen Elizabeth I of England, Joan of Arc and Isabelle of Spain but had also multiplied these virtues in herself to an infinite degree. The Minister of Public Health, Ramon Carillo, ordered a 220-lb candle, the height of Evita (5ft 5in) to be installed in the Ministry and lighted for an hour on the 26th day of every month (the day Evita died). Carillo thought the candle would last 100 years or more. The Argentine Post Office ordered the printing of new stamps of all denominations bearing the picture of Eva Perón and prohibited the sale of any other stamps for a year. Argentines throughout the world, including the athletes who were at the Olympic Games in Finland, were told to wear black bands of mourning, and all members of the Perónista Party were ordered to wear black ties at party functions for the rest of their lives. Even the children were caught up in the frenzy. The Feminist Perónista Party asked the government to build an 'Eva Perón shrine' in all schools so that 'children may slake their thirst for knowledge of the works of this great woman.' Schools were given prizes to be distributed to children who wrote the best poems and essays praising Evita.

But there were indications that the country was not unanimous in its mourning. At the University of La Plata, not far from Buenos Aires, students burned a crepe hanging in front of their dining room door. When the dean directed that as an act of penance all students wishing to use the restaurant, which had special low prices, would have to wear black ties and armbands, the students simply stayed away from school for a week — a pretty mild and harmless expression of protest. But anything more outspoken would certainly have drawn down the wrath of outraged Perónistas on their heads. As it was there were numerous examples of petty nastiness against those who did not show sufficient respect or fervour in their mourning. Carlos Aloe, the fanatical Governor of Buenos Aires Province, fired an employee who refused to wear a black tie. A Buenos Aires youth was arrested for laughing on a street car. The director of one of the city's major hospitals was dismissed for lack of respect because he had continued to work during the mourning period. 'Attitudes like these are anti-social,' said Aloe.

But the frenzied scenes around the Ministry of Labour had apparently scared even many devoted Perónistas. When the body was moved August 9th to the National Congress Building, a great segment of the city's populace stayed away from the mile-long processional route. At regular intervals, the State

Radio pleaded with its listeners to get out on to the deserted streets and watch the mournful parade. Evita, in fact, was being given all the full military honours that normally in Argentina are accorded to a president who dies in office. As an army band began to play Chopin's Funeral March, troops lined two deep along the 14-block route from the Ministry of Labour to the Congress presented arms. Behind a detachment of mounted grenadiers, three files of men and women workers in white shirts and black trousers drew an ancient gun carriage on which was mounted the tiny, silver-encrusted, mahogany coffin. Following right behind, President Perón led the cortege of mourners — Cabinet Ministers, members of Congress, labour leaders, and senior officers of the armed forces. On each side marched files of cadet nurses from the Eva Perón Foundation, students, workers, and leaders of the Peronista Feminist Party.

Evita remained at the Congress Building for only one day, a Snow White-like figure, dressed in a flowing white tunic, her blonde hair resting neatly on a small white pillow, looking as though all she needed was a kiss from one of her faithful descamisados to bring her to life. The next day the workers came for her. But first the nation's top political leaders delivered themselves of a final outpouring of oratorical grief. Interior Minister Angel G. Borlenghi described Evita as the 'martyr of labour, protecting saint, haven for the humble, sun of the aged, and good fairy to the children.' Always considering herself as the equal of the most humble, Señora Perón fought to improve their lot and gave not charity but justice to the poor, he continued. 'In the orchestra of government, Eva Perón was the diapason of justicialist purity — the pure gold. She was the tuning fork to sound any government measure. If she was happy with it the people would be happy with it, too. If she was mild so also the people. If she rejected it the people would reject it: She was the quintessence of the people's feeling.' With her passing the task that had devolved upon the people was to serve General Perón unconditionally, Señor Borlenghi declared. Placing a hand on the coffin and gazing down at the still figure, he concluded: 'We swear for our fatherland and you, Eva Perón, to continue struggling to be loyal to Perón and to give our lives to Perón.'

Other speakers were equally flowery. Dr Rudolfo Valenzuela, speaking for the Argentine Supreme Court, described Evita as having possessed 'the unbreakable faith of the missionary, the unbending courage of the fanatical soldier, the overwhelming passion of the politician and the suave tenderness of the woman

165

in love.' Argentine justice would be guided by the tenets she held and demonstrated, he promised. Then Juana Larrauri, Evita's right-hand woman in the Feminist Party, sobbed out: 'For us you have not died. You are the eternal burning torch, guiding us on our way.' Finally, the small coffin was once again carried out into the street, mounted on a gun carriage and drawn by fifty workers through two miles of the city's main streets to the headquarters of the National Confederation of Labour near the waterfront. Unlike the day before, this time the route was lined by hundreds of thousands of sorrowing, weeping Argentines. Two CGT floats bearing flaming torches and the slogan, 'The flame of your memory will forever live in our hearts', preceded the coffin with the workers on them strewing flowers and petals in front of the wheels of the gun carriage. Yet more flowers rained down from the packed windows of the buildings lining the path of the cortege. As it drew up to the wreath-covered entrance to the labour headquarters, a 21-gun salute thundered out and Lincoln bombers and Meteor jets streaked low overhead.

As Juan Perón, his face etched with the lines of grief, handed over the body of his wife to CGT Secretary-General Jose Espejo, he must have known as he looked down at her that he was parting with her share of his power. If he did not, then Espejo made it clear right then and there. On the steps of the magnificent union headquarters that Evita had built, Espejo promised: 'Upon receiving the remains of Eva Perón, I swear to be their custodian today, tomorrow and forever.' Anyone knowing Espejo knew that this was more a threat than rhetoric. His words carried the plain implication that from now on, anyone, including President Perón himself, who sought to curb the CGT leadership and the spoils of the Eva Perón Foundation would have to take on the guardians of Evita — the theory being that in a crisis her corpse could generate far more political magic with the Argentine people than a living Juan Perón. He had inherited a myth which in the years to come he was going to find impossible to live with.

14

SAINT EVITA?

On August 1, 1952, the union of food workers cabled Pope Pius XII asking 'in the name of 160,000 members that Your Holiness initiate the process of canonisation of Eva Perón.' To support this request, the union told of a little girl paying her last respects, who said: 'Eva was a saint. I know because she cured my mother.' It added: 'Many sick are now well, many sorrowful are happy because of her.' The Vatican response was quick, smooth, and predictable. 'While in the case of Señora de Perón the civic virtues were practised in an evident way,' said a Vatican spokesman, choosing his words carefully, 'nothing is known about her religious virtues, and, at first sight, there seems not to have been any of the heroism required by the church in such matters.'

The church, it appeared, did not seem to believe that a woman who had known as many lovers as Evita before marriage was quite suitable material for sainthood. But it did not really matter. She already was a saint to hundreds of thousands of elderly Argentine women around the country who had set up shrines to her in their homes. The government, too, was planning a shrine — the world's biggest. Her embalmed remains were to be kept permanently on view in a crypt patterned after Napoleon's tomb which was to be topped by a 450-foot statue of a descamisado in Carrara marble. But while Italian sculptors

167

chipped away on that four-year project, in Buenos Aires the Evita legend seemed to be quietly but rapidly receding into the mists of history. More than two months after her death, the Association of Friends of Eva Perón', founded in the first hour of grief by high-placed Perónistas, had yet to hold its first meeting. The film *Evita Immortal*, released shortly after her death, had been withdrawn from circulation after only a short run. Press and radio had drastically reduced the amount of time and space devoted to her. The President himself never mentioned her name in public speeches anymore. It looked as though the widower in the Casa Rosada was trying to exorcise the ghost around him.

Nine months after Evita Peron died, her brother, Juan Duarte, her adored Juancito, was dead, too, found in his bedroom with a bullet in the brain, a gun beside him. Officially it was a suicide. But when his mother, Juana Ibarguren, heard the news she screamed, 'He has murdered my two children.' Word of her outburst spread like lightning through the city. There was no doubting at whom she was pointing the finger. Only three days before, Peron had forced his brother-in-law to resign as his private secretary after publicly stating that he would imprison any dishonest official even if it happened to be his own father (who had died when he was a child).

There was no Evita to protect Juan Duarte this time, or to save the other men she had so carefully placed in positions of power. Jose Espejo was already gone from the CGT, fired within weeks of his emotional outburst over her coffin when he swore to be the custodian of her bones for ever. Hector Campora, her loyal servant in Congress, had been forced to resign as President of the Chamber of Deputies. Jose Maria Freyre, her hand-picked Minister of Labour, had also been ousted. And Evita's enemies were returning to positions of power even as Dr Ara put the finishing touches to her immortality in his laboratory at CGT headquarters.

In fact, Duarte was doomed from the moment that the new CGT General Secretary, Eduardo Vuletich, arrived at a Cabinet meeting arm-in-arm with Minister of Defence, General Sosa Molina, who had never forgotten or forgiven his humiliation at Evita's hands. Vuletich complained about the corruption spreading through the country and accused the President's private secretary of using the power of his position to enrich himself. When another Cabinet minister offered a timid defence

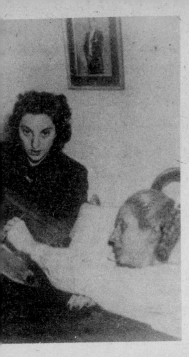

Above: Voting for her husband from her sick bed in the Presidential election, November 11, 1951.

Below: Evita's last public appearance as Juan Perón takes the Presidential oath of office, June 4, 1952.

Queueing in the pouring rain to see Evita's body lying in state in the Minist
of Labour after her death, July 26, 1952.

The whole nation seemed crazed with grief.

Flowers piled 20 feet high up the side of the Ministry's walls.

For 16 years Evita's body lay in this Milan grave.

Reunited: Juan and Evita side by side in the Presidential chapel in Olivos, December 10, 1974.

Finally laid to rest, October 22, 1976, in the Duarte tomb in Recoleta cemetery, Buenos Aires.

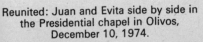

Evita: in life and death.

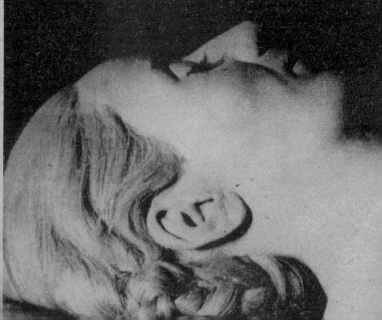

of Duarte, General Sosa Molina ordered him to shut up. Then, for the next couple of hours, Perón was given a detailed account of how his brother-in-law had put together a fortune worth twelve million pounds according to some estimates — quite an accomplishment for a man who only nine years earlier had been earning £12 a month as a soap salesman.

Perón expressed shock and fury, though he had only himself to blame if he really was ignorant of what had been going on. With the press muzzled and criticism a passport to gaol, a dictator only hears what the men around him want him to hear. But Perón must have known what Duarte was up to. Dr Ivan Ivanessevich, an old friend who had taken out his appendix and had also written his party's marching song, the 'Perónista Boys', recalled twenty years later how he had resigned as Minister of Education and had taken the boat to Uruguay when he discovered that businessmen had to bribe Juan Duarte in order to see the President. But Perón had not been at all shocked when he told him at the time. 'Look Ivan,' the surgeon remembered his President telling him, 'the British Empire was built by good men and pirates and I'm going to build the Argentine empire with good men and pirates.'

But Juan Duarte was a pirate whose time had come to walk the plank. For Perón had a score to settle with him. Soon after Evita's death, the President discovered that his wife had for three years before her death systematically dispatched suitcases full of jewellery and cash worth possibly six million pounds to a bank vault in Switzerland. He sent Duarte off to Europe, either to find the key of the bank vault or to persuade the Swiss to transfer the fortune to his name. Under Argentine law, he was supposed to divide that wealth with Evita's mother. Duarte, however, carried with him a power of attorney from Perón — a document signed by the President of the Supreme Court certifying that Evita's mother had waived all rights to her estate. Accompanied by Hector Campora, he was gone a month, but returned without any apparent success. Then, in April of 1953, just 24 hours before the Cabinet confrontation, Duarte was betrayed by a jilted girl friend, Maliza Zini, one of the many actresses whose company he kept in Buenos Aires. She got word to Perón that his brother-in-law had 'liquidated' a great deal of Evita's jewellery while in Europe. She added bitterly that he had given a temporary girl friend a gem worth £2,500 while staying at the Excelsior Hotel in Rome.

Perón demanded and received Duarte's resignation during the

Cabinet meeting. Reading the signs, Evita's brother decided it was time to clear out. He drove to the airport to catch a plane to Spain. But the police were waiting for him and took his passport away. Then he tried in vain to rent a motor launch to escape across the river to Montevideo. The next evening he had friends in for dinner at his apartment: Dr Raul Margueirate, chief of protocol at the Foreign Ministry, Raul Apold, sub-secretary of Press and Information, and his personal doctor. They stayed with him until 12.30. The next day, at 7 o'clock, the Minister of Industry, Rafael Amundarain, arrived at Duarte's apartment and found him lying across his bed in a dressing gown, a bullet through his skull.

The medical examination by the police established that death was caused by a .45 automatic, a weapon used by the army and police. He had died sometime between 12.30 and 2 am. Perón was told at 10 o'clock and paid a short visit six hours later to the bier of the man who had been his private secretary for seven years. But Juan Duarte's mother was not at the wake. Nor was her name mentioned in the official condolences. The official announcement that the death was a suicide was made later that day, and the next morning Duarte was buried. It was only then that a police surgeon quietly let it be known that the bullet had been fired from such a distance as to rule out suicide. Another bit of information slipped out: the dead man's office had been ransacked on the morning of his death by federal agents. No reasons were given. Presumably the agents were looking for the keys of Evita's vault in Switzerland.

The President did not attend Juan Duarte's funeral. He had other crises to cope with — high prices, meat shortages, corruption. The country was sinking deeply into an economic quagmire. And without Evita he was lost. He could still produce the words in that deep, rich voice, vibrating and echoing around the plaza. In earlier days that would have been enough to send the crowds away laughing and contented. 'Corruption,' he snorted, 'the administration has always had these small abnormalities of disposing of more revenue than has been estimated.' High prices! 'Look,' he lectured, 'I can't have enough police to take care of eighteen million dunces who let themselves be robbed.' But the rhetoric was not enough. He could not talk away the discontent, although he tried wilder, more hysterical demagoguery, and his police filled the gaols with those who complained.

But now his enemies were doing more than just complaining.

The weekend before Juan Duarte's death, two bombs exploded in the Plaza de Mayo as the President spoke to thousands of his faithful descamisados massed below. Six people were killed by the blasts or were crushed to death in the stampeding, terrified crowd. Perón pleaded with them to stay calm. But then he seemed to be carried away by the frenzy of the moment. 'Go out and club them, hang them,' he shrieked. Obediently, his supporters poured through the city streets. No one died. But the Jockey Club, the palatial five-storey building on Calle Florida, the symbol of the country's aristocracy, was burnt to the ground, wiping out one of the finest art collections and libraries in the nation and a wine cellar considered South America's best. The headquarters of the opposition Radical and Socialist Parties were also set to the torch, the petrol supplied by teams of brown-shirted youths wearing the arm-bands of the fascist National Alliance while federal police looked the other way.

That was not Evita's style. She preferred to humiliate the aristocracy, getting her beloved descamisados to hoot with laughter with her as she stank the members of the Jockey Club out of their fortress by placing a fish stall in front of the club in the height of summer the year before she died.

But it was more than her street-wise guile that was gone. She had ruled the Casa Rosada and the country with a fierce passion. Even in her last illness, she had still been able to summon up short bursts of the temper that had made Cabinet Ministers tremble. She even raged at Perón at times. 'Whenever he feels down in spirits, I kick him up,' she once said. She fought his natural indolence and her driving spirit forced him on. Without her, he became in no time at all an old fashioned run-of-the-mill Latin American military dictator, relying on the violence of his followers to curb his enemies while he indulged in the pastimes he had been forced to abandon from the day he met Evita.

He had cut his Presidential office duties to the morning hours and was usually on his way home to the Olivos residence by noon. He had turned the eucalyptus-shaded estate into a recreation centre for high school girls. 'Just call me *Pocho*,' he told the girls. Crews of workers added tennis and basketball courts, a swimming pool, open-air theatre and riding stables. So that the girls could go to the nearby river beach without crossing a busy street, Perón had a costly tunnel dug.

He spent hours watching the girls play basketball, and he would ride around the grounds with them on scooters, which for ever after in Buenos Aires were known as *pochonetas*. He also

171

let them use the mansion as a clubhouse. 'It's too big for a lone man like me,' he said. He was not lonely for long. A pretty thirteen-year-old brunette named Nelly Rivas caught his eye and she soon became his mistress in a love nest he had built in the basement of the Olivos mansion. He showered her with jewels and built a small concrete house in the suburbs for her parents (years later when friends asked him how he could have defiled the memory of Evita with a thirteen-year-old, he joked, 'So she was thirteen. I'm not superstitious').

Rumours of sex orgies behind the high walls of the presidential mansion spread like wildfire through the country. Perhaps more than anything else the stories shocked middle and upper class Argentines into a determination to rid themselves of Perón. However, there was little they could do as long as the army supported the President. But then Perón made an error that eventually proved to be fatal. He attacked the Roman Catholic Church, whose faithful numbered ninety per cent of Argentina's population. It was a move that Evita never would have allowed. Although she had never had any love for the church, she respected its power. She had always seen to it that a priest was on hand to deliver the invocation at rallies of her descamisados. She had pushed legislation to make catholic religious instruction compulsory in the schools, and she never went anywhere without her priest, Father Benitez. But after her death, many young Argentine priests had joined anti-Perónist organisations in protest against increasing repression. What particularly incensed Perón, however, was that catholics had begun to play bigger roles in the trade unions. He bluntly warned the church to lay off. And he followed this with more specific reprisals. He put through legislation legalising divorce and prostitution in a manner calculated to cause maximum affront to the church. His police arrested dozens of priests for desacato, disrespect, and he suspended religious teaching in the schools.

Events moved rapidly towards a confrontation. In defiance of a government ban, 100,000 catholics marched into his own Plaza de Mayo, which the Casa Rosada shares with the city's main cathedral. As mounted police charged the crowd, groups of priests in ranks of four and five deep on the cathedral steps chanted, 'Long Live Christ the King.' On the following day, Perón, in a countrywide radio address, called the ecclesiastic hierarchy a 'wolf in sheep's clothing'. He added: . . . 'I do not know if this patient Argentine people may not one day . . . take justice into its own hand.' Two bishops, accused of organising

172

the catholic march, were hustled aboard a plane for Rome. On Thursday, June 16, 1955, the Vatican answered by imposing on Perón the most dreadful spiritual penalty within its power: excommunication for him and all others in his regime who had 'trampled' on church rights and 'used violence' against a bishop.

News of the Vatican action reached Buenos Aires at about 11 am. Within two hours, Argentina's bloodiest revolution in over half a century had started. It began dramatically as noonday crowds strolled in Plaza de Mayo. A wave of aircraft dived out of an overcast sky and dropped their bombs on the Casa Rosada, which Perón had left a few minutes earlier for the Army Ministry building a few blocks away. Then rebel sailors who had gathered in the nearby Naval Ministry attacked the Casa Rosada with machine gun fire. As army trucks filled with khaki-clad troops loyal to Perón rolled into the plaza, the planes swooped over again, dropping another load of bombs that landed in the plaza. But the revolt was all but over.

Only an hour later a white flag fluttered up over the Navy building. Most of the dead were civilians caught in the crossfire and the bombing. Their bodies, 400 of them, lay scattered across the plaza. That night, in revenge, Perónista mobs swept through Buenos Aires, setting fire to catholic churches.

Three months later, on Friday September 16, rebellion broke out again at several points in Argentina, beginning in Cordoba where students and revolutionary army units battled loyal Perónista regiments. Simultaneously, the Navy steamed out of its bases and sailed on Buenos Aires, threatening to bombard the city if Perón did not surrender. Four days later, he fled to sanctuary aboard a Paraguayan gunboat undergoing repairs in Buenos Aires harbour, pencilling a goodbye note to Nelly Rivas: 'My dear baby girl . . . I miss you every day, as I do my little dogs . . . Many kisses and many desires. Until I see you soon, Papi.' 'He loved me,' Nelly insisted. 'He could have been my grandfather, but he loved me. He always told me I was very pretty, but I'm not really, am I?'

Anti-Perónistas, silent, pent-up for ten years, burst out into the streets waving flags, embracing one another, laughing, cheering, chanting 'Long live liberty,' repeating the phrase again and again as though they hardly believed it was true. Perónista party centres were attacked and pictures of the hated dictator and his dead wife were ripped off walls and buildings and burnt. Statues of Santa Evita were toppled and dragged through the streets to be kicked and spat upon. Two thirty-ton marble statues of Juan and Evita on top of the new Grecian-style Eva Perón Foundation (handed over to the university of Buenos Aires) were covered in black cloth and then cut up for use by students. The site of Evita's crypt and monument was dynamited and turned into a children's paddling pool. The provinces of Presidente Perón and Eva Perón reverted to their original names of El Chaco and La Pampa. Eva Perón City once again became La Plata. In the seaside resort of Mar del Plata, crowds destroyed a flower bed dedicated to Evita and arranged as a clock set at 8.25, the time she died. They attacked and wrecked the Seventeenth of October Hotel, which she had built for workers' holidays, and tore down a giant portrait of her in the foyer. Political prisoners were released from gaol, and the new military government dispatched a cruiser to Montevideo to bring home the exiles.

There was no resistance from the workers, although they had promised Evita to give their lives for Perón and two weeks before the revolution an order had gone out from CGT headquarters that 'in the event of a revolt and the defeat of General Perón, a general strike will be implemented, effective until restoration.' Evita's newspaper, *Democracia*, in its final issue warned the military that 'the people will wait with passionate confidence for the banner of that October.' But it was meaningless rhetoric. The workers did not march into Buenos Aires as they had on that October 17th ten years before. They were unarmed and they faced soldiers prepared to kill. So, instead, the workers obeyed the military government which ordered all of them to be at their place of work as usual or be declared saboteurs, subject to the penalties of martial law, which included death. In the working-class barrios and slums, women contented themselves with the thought that 'Evita's tears' — the worst thunderstorm in living memory — helped Perón to escape capture and almost certain death as he slipped through the military cordon around the city docks to board the Paraguayan gunboat that took him into exile.

He found a haven in a succession of Latin American dictatorships — Alfred Stroessner's Paraguay, Anastasio Somoza's Nicaragua, Marcos Perez Jimenez's Venezuela, and Rafael Trujillo's Dominican Republic — before settling in Francisco Franco's Spain. The military leaders who replaced him in Argentina swore he would never come back. To discredit him in the eyes of his followers, they opened up his homes for public viewing so that Argentines could see for themselves how the

174

leader of the descamisados had lived. The treasure trove included Evita's breathtaking and priceless collection of jewellery, his 16 custom-built sports cars of every famous foreign make, his 240 scooters, and cupboards crammed with hundreds of suits and uniforms. Police said they had found £5 million in cash in various safes in the two Presidential mansions, the San Vicente quinta, and two apartments, one of them a love-nest with bedrooms lined with mirrors and carpeted with white bearskin rugs. Over a well-stocked bar was written the mocking slogan: 'Someone always gets assaulted when a poor man has some fun.' To further disgrace Perón, a military court tried him in absentia for his love affair with Nelly Rivas, stripping him of his rank of general for 'conduct unworthy of an officer and a gentleman'. Delivering their verdict, the judges wrote 'It is superfluous to stress the stupor of the court at the proof of such a crime committed by one who has always claimed that the only privileged in the land were children.'

Discrediting Evita was much harder. The new regime displayed her jewels, and her dresses and furs. But that made little impression on Argentine workers because she had never hidden them. In fact, she had flaunted them, knowing that she was the glittering Cinderella princess of the descamisados, the embodiment of their hopes and dreams. The generals worried that her body, lying in CGT headquarters, would become the centre of a Perón cult in the way that bodies had become national symbols before in Argentine history. Some senior officers suggested it should be burnt and the ashes thrown into the Riachuelo River. Others wanted to drop the body from a naval aircraft out over the Atlantic. However, Dr Ara, Evita's embalmer, who had made himself the guardian of the body during the turmoil of Perón's overthrow, told the army that it was imperishable. It could not be burnt or drowned. But three months after the revolution the body disappeared. It was not seen again for sixteen years.

Even without the body — or perhaps because of its very absence — the mass of Argentine people did not forget. The cult of Saint Evita flourished, dooming every attempt by the nation's generals to return the government to stable civilian rule. Posters of an ethereal Evita plastered the walls of every town and village in the country. Working-class families kept her picture in their homes, although doing so was grounds for arrest. The wall signs demanded 'Return Evita to us', and the generals responded with repression. They purged — even executed — leading Perónistas. They outlawed Perónism as a political movement and demolished the Perónista trade unions. They never hesitated to cancel a ballot or stage a coup whenever Perón's supporters won elections, which they always did when given the chance to vote for their own candidates.

No matter what course the generals followed — repression or persuasion — they could not root out the memory among millions of Argentines that it was Perón and Evita who had given them a place of respect in their country. As a building worker remembered it: 'In this country under Perón a worker spoke as loudly as the factory manager. Now,' he added, 'we have nobody to defend us.' Reminded that Perón was a corrupt demagogue who ran a police state totally lacking in basic democratic freedoms, Perónistas responded that they had enjoyed the highest standard of living working people had ever known in their country's history. 'When I got married in 1948, my wife and I were so poor that a sip of milk was a luxury,' recalled Saturnino Astorga, a stockyard worker, who spoke to *Newsweek* magazine reporter Milan J. Kubic in 1964, nine years after Perón's overthrow. 'We couldn't spare a few pence each month for a bus ride to visit her parents. Then came Perón. Evita gave me this house. My salary jumped fivefold. We lived like people. Thanks to the Peróns', Astorga said, 'he was able to buy furniture and a refrigerator, his sons went to government-built schools and ate cheap lunches at government-subsidised cafeterias, his whole family enjoyed a fifteen-day paid holiday, and their medical bills were paid by the state. None of the politicians who followed Perón have done anything for me,' he said. 'I am 100 per cent Perónista and always will be.'

A succession of military governments could not reduce that stubborn faith. The years passed. The signs scrawled on the walls got larger — 'Where is Eva Perón's Body?' 'Give Back the Body of the Beloved Señora.' The paint stayed fresh. Terrorists killed in her name. Bombs exploded like firecrackers on the anniversary of her death. A former President, General Pedro Aramburu, who had taken power soon after Perón was overthrown, was kidnapped and murdered in a vain attempt to make him tell where Evita's body had been hidden. The nation hovered on the brink of civil war. The economy crumbled. Shops went bankrupt. Unemployment skyrocketed, and coup followed coup as one military moustache (as Argentines sardonically call their generals) followed another through the revolving door of the presidential palace. Finally, in 1972, the generals capitulated and decided it was time for Perón to come home. But first they gave him back the body of his wife. In Lot 86, Garden 41 in Musocco Cemetery in Milan, Italy, the body of Maria Maggi, an Italian woman who had died in Argentina , was exhumed. The coffin's black wooden casing was rotting. But the corpse was in excellent condition. It was the embalmed body of Evita Perón.

It had wandered far and lain in strange places over the years. On that December evening in 1955 when it disappeared, the head of the Argentine army's intelligence service, Colonel Carlos Mori-Koenig led a detail of troops into CGT headquarters on a mission for which they were all sworn to secrecy. They found what they were looking for in room 63. The body lay in total darkness on a bier covered with a blue and white Argentine flag. Colonel Mori-Koenig told the marine guards on duty that he had been ordered by President Aramburu to give it a Christian burial. It was put into a cheap wooden coffin and carried out to an army truck. There it remained, parked overnight, while the colonel waited for further instructions. But President Aramburu had still not made up his mind what to do with the body. He told the army intelligence chief to keep it hidden. For a while it was kept in the apartment of Mori-Koenig's deputy, Major Antonio Arandia.

Perónistas, aroused to fury by the disappearance of their saint, sent out their own agents on a clandestine hunt for the body. Fearful that the secret of his silent guest might leak out, the major took to sleeping with his service revolver under his pillow. One morning, before dawn, he was awakened by strange noises in the corridor outside his bedroom. He shot twice at a form that appeared in the doorway, killing his pregnant wife who had gone to the bathroom. After that, Evita's body was moved to the fourth floor of military intelligence headquarters and dumped in a packing case labelled 'radio sets'.

At that point, Colonel Hector Cabanillas, the head of the Casa Rosada secret service, took over responsibility for the body, the President having finally decided to send it abroad until passions in Argentina cooled. In September of 1956, the body, still in its packing case marked 'radio sets', was shipped to the Argentine Embassy in Bonn, where it was kept in the storeroom, unknown to the Ambassador. It was then put in a coffin and shipped to Rome, where it was met by a lay sister of the Society of St Paul named Giuseppina Airoldi, who had been told that the body was that of an Italian widow who died in Argentina having left instructions for her burial in her home town of Milan. There, under the name of Maggi, Evita was laid to rest.

On September 2, 1971, a man describing himself as Carlos Maggi, brother of the fictitious Maria, appeared at the cemetery with written permission to exhume his sister's remains. He was, in fact, none other than former intelligence chief Hector Cabanillas, who had long since retired from military service. He looked worried and in a desperate hurry as the body was placed in a hearse hired from a Milan undertaker. There was good reason for his concern. Word had been received from Buenos Aires that a Perónista terrorist group had sent agents to Italy to search for the body. If they got their hands on it they would certainly use it as a symbol in their guerrilla war against the Argentine army, a war that had already cost hundreds of lives. Failure by Cabanillas to return the body to Perón would doom the military regime's attempt to bring about a national reconciliation.

The Argentine Government sought the cooperation of the Italian, French and Spanish Governments. As the hearse raced across Europe with its precious cargo, it was waved across national borders without the usual customs check. After spending the night in a Perpignan garage, Cabanillas drove into Spain and was escorted by two car loads of Spanish police on the final 450 mile lap to Madrid. At nine o'clock that evening, he passed through the gates of 6 Calle de Navalmanzano in the fashionable Puerto de Heirro suburb of Madrid. Waiting at the front door for him were Juan Perón, his new young wife, Isabel, whom he had met in a nightclub in Panama during his early days of exile, and Dr Pedro Ara, who had embalmed Evita nineteen years before.

They carried the coffin into the house. Cabanillas prised open the lid. For the first time in sixteen years, Perón gazed down on the face of his beloved Evita. Dr Ara recalled the moment in his posthumously published memoirs. 'Without the least disorder in her coiffure, her hair appeared wet and dirty,' he wrote. 'The stainless steel hairpins, now rusted, crumbled in our fingers. The General's wife began unbinding Eva's braids to air and dry her hair and to clean it of dirt and rust.' While Perón looked on, Isabel and Dr Ara cut away her stained white tunic. A fingertip had been broken off. One ear was slightly bent. But other than that and a few minor cracks in the plastic coating, the body was

178

in the same condition as the professor had seen it last in 1955. As he had promised Perón on the morning after Evita's death, she had remained incorruptible.

She was left behind in Madrid when Perón returned to Argentina the following year, invited home by the people she had hated with such passion — the military leaders, large landowners, big businessmen who thought he could heal the wounds that had bled their country for so many years. At the age of 77, he was still a commanding presence, the jet black hair dyed but as thick as ever, his six-foot, 200-pound frame ramrod straight, and a smile as dazzling as the summer pampas sun. His booming, spellbinding voice still filled the plaza, and the Argentine people flocked back to his banner in greater numbers than ever before. He was re-elected President with seven million votes, a 62 per cent majority. And this time his wife was elected Vice-President without any argument from the army. But he was too old. Perhaps he had always lacked Evita's passion, and without it and her he was lost. 'I'm a vegetarian lion,' he once said sadly. He was unable to provide the vigorous leadership his country so desperately needed, and he could not put a stop to violent feuding between the right and left wings of his party.

He soon aligned himself with the right-wingers, the old trade union leaders of his earlier years. The young Perónistas who shouted 'If Evita lived, she'd be a Montonera' (guerrilla), he dismissed as 'jerks'. But to the party's youngsters, who were born after Evita's death, it was the dead Perón, not the ageing *caudillo* in the Palace, who symbolised the radical revolution they sought for Argentina. It seemed an unlikely union. Evita was a materialist who believed in homes for the workers and jewels for herself, and it was hard to believe that she would have shown any sympathy for the youthful middle-class university-educated revolutionaries (the Montoneros in Argentina, the Tupermaros in Uruguay, and the MIR in Chile) whose mindless violence provoked the overthrow of democracies and the vicious repression of workers by military regimes in all three countries.

On July 1, 1974, the Buenos Aires morning newspaper *Critica* carried a headline that filled half the front page. 'MURIO', he is dead. Once again hundreds of thousands of Argentines lined up eight abreast in the winter rain to bid farewell to a Perón. They waited for up to 24 hours for a glimpse of his body which lay in state in the Blue Chamber of Congress, clad in army uniform, medals and sash of office. Men and women burst into tears. There were cries of 'Adios, *mi General*' and 'Chau, *viejo*, goodbye old man. And there was repeated chanting of 'Perón esta presente', Perón is here, a rephrasing of the cry that was heard twenty-two years before at Evita's death.

It was time for her to come home. Perón's widow, Isabel, now President of Argentina in his place, sent a chartered jetliner for her. But it was a return journey that was almost as strange as the rest of Evita's odyssey in death. The body was escorted by Isabel's Social Welfare Minister, Jose Lopez Rega, an astrologer and mystic who claimed daily communication with the Angel Gabriel. When the plane arrived in Buenos Aires, the ever-faithful descamisados were kept at bay outside the airport while Lopez Rega and a dozen bodyguards carrying submachine guns loaded the coffin on a carriage and rushed it off to the presidential residence in Olivos. There it lay alongside Perón's coffin in the crypt of the presidential chapel while Isabel and Lopez Rega worked on plans to build a giant 160-foot high Altar of the Fatherland that was to be the final resting place for Evita and her General and all the other divisive ghosts in Argentina's history. A law was signed authorising the return of the bones of the country's first dictator, Juan Manal Rosas from the catholic cemetery in Southampton. 'Linked in glory', read the planned motto, 'we watch over the destinies of the fatherland. Let no man use our memory to divide the Argentines.'

But it was not to be. Isabel Perón was no Evita. She clung to power for two years with the help of the death squads of the Argentine Anti-Communist Alliance (the Triple A) which her friend Lopez Rega organised to purge her opponents through multiple assassinations. On March 24, 1976, with the country nearing 1,000 per cent inflation and a civil war, the generals seized power again in Argentina. Isabel Perón they goaled. Evita they buried.

EPILOGUE

In 1977, the Peróns are not only dead, they are non-persons. Anyone found writing their names on a street wall is killed on the spot. At the national archives, officials will not release pictures of Evita without the signed permission of the Minister of the Interior, which is never given. 'You have to understand,' said an embarrassed clerk, 'she is politically sensitive.' A student caught with a cassette of the musical *Evita* was thrown into gaol as a 'subversive'. He was really more stupid than subversive, for few Argentines would risk smuggling a copy of the record into the country. It is not officially banned. But the head of the record company which would have imported *Evita* received a phone call from a high-ranking army officer in the government who said he had just called to express the hope that the company would not be handling that particular label. The executive assured him, with sincerity, that he had not even considered the idea. As he told a friend later, 'What does he think I am, crazy?' Public association with those long ago days of Juan and Eva can be an invitation for a kidnapping and a bullet in the head.

All that Evita accomplished for her beloved descamisados has been wiped out by the military regime headed by General Jorge Rafael Videla. Workers' wages in real terms are not much more than half of what they were in her day. The CGT is run by senior military officers. Many trade union leaders have been kidnapped and murdered. Industrial companies have been told to report 'trouble-makers' so that they can be dealt with. As *The Times* pointed out in a strongly-worded editorial on September 9, 1977, Argentina 'is in the grip of an extremist regime which is waging a war of terror against anyone it suspects of opposing its ideas.' In Evita's time, Villa Devoto gaol became an unpleasant home away from home for many of her political opponents who were not prepared to take the boat into exile. But they all came out alive. Now, month after month, hundreds of people are carried off from their homes by armed men belonging to the government's multitude of security agencies. They become desaparecidos, missing people. Thousands have been tortured and murdered. The victims range from the two-year-old grandson of a newspaper editor who had himself been kidnapped and murdered to a 63-year-old grandmother seized on the streets of her home town. Each day, newspapers run appeals from parents who plead that they only want to know if their children are still alive, like 'Margarita Erlich, a 26-year-old fine arts student, who was taken from her home at Pueyrredon 2458 (10-A) on April 6, 1976 by five heavily armed men who claimed to be from the federal police. Her parents have filed some ten writs of habeas corpus, sent more than 100 letters and telegrams and are now making a public appeal for help in locating Margarita and ending their days of anguish and searching.'

In Evita's time Argentines were not afraid to walk the streets of their capital. Now it is commonplace to read that 'two young women were forced into two automobiles and driven away by armed men yesterday afternoon from the corner of Cordoba Avenue and San Martin Street in the heart of the Buenos Aires business district. Many people watched astonishedly as the women were taken from a hotel located in San Martin between Viamonte and Cordoba at 3.45 pm. The men, dressed in civilian clothes and armed with 45 calibre pistols, forced the women into two cars. Despite their screams, no one helped the two women. One screamed that her name was Diana Garcia and asked that someone call the police as she had no idea why she was being kidnapped.' No one interfered primarily because to do so could mean instant death and also because Argentines have become hardened to such scenes.

On crowded Corrientes, where Evita first sought her fame and fortune behind theatre footlights, no one gives a second glance to the green Ford Falcon with its hooded passenger in the back as it screeches through traffic and red lights.

In Pilar, a village near Buenos Aires, residents were woken just before dawn by the sound of vehicles stopping on the highway. Voices were heard, ordering people out of the vehicles. Then screams were heard, followed by the sound of automatic fire. After a few minutes of silence, an explosion was heard and then the vehicles sped away.

In the first morning light, local farmers found the remains of thirty men and women, desaparecidos, who had been taken from their gaol cells and slaughtered in revenge for the murder by guerrillas the day before of a retired general. A sign by the bodies said: 'Montonero cemetery, killed as enemies of the nation.'

Yet most middle-class Argentines shrug off such atrocities with the comment that desaparecidos were 'involved', that they could not have been picked up for nothing. And the country's military leaders have excused what President Videla admits as 'an excess of repression by the forces of order' on the grounds that Argentina is 'waging a war against the destructive gospel of totalitarianism'. But as an editorial in the English-language

Buenos Aires Herald pointed out after the murder of five priests who worked in the slums of Buenos Aires, it has 'become increasingly clear to every law abiding person in Argentina — unless blinkered by prejudice — that some mindless Frankenstein's monster has gone beserk.' Few newspapers in Argentina have dared to speak out so openly. For while Evita bought up or closed down newspapers that opposed her, the current Argentine press has been cowed into silence by a worse threat. For the list is long of newsmen who have been kidnapped and murdered, and there has been none of the outrage displayed by the world press after the closing of *La Prensa*. To add to the horror, the latent anti-semitism that wells to the surface in periods of turmoil in Argentina has shown itself in the bombing of synagogues and the disappearance of whole Jewish families. One central police station in Buenos Aires has had a large swastika painted over the cell block entrance. Lawyers, women as well as men, who have had the courage to defend captured or suspected guerrillas, have been accused of complicity for doing so and have been kidnapped, tortured and murdered.

But life goes on in one of the world's great capitals as though, on the surface, anyway, nothing out of the ordinary had happened. The opera, theatres, and restaurants are crowded at night. Porteños stroll through Calle Florida at midnight, past book stores and record shops that are still open for business. The soccer stadiums are full at weekends and so are the rugger fields and tennis courts. The economy is back in the hands of the landed aristocracy. Dr Jose Alfredo Martinez de Hoz, the Minister of Economy who reduced the country's crippling inflation rate from 486 percent to 150 percent in one year, was educated at Eton and is one of the richest men in Latin America. The great pampas is once again producing an unending amount of cereals and meat for a hungry world. The guerrilla organisations — the Montoneros and the People's Revolutionary Army (ERP) — every bit as brutal and murderous as the right-wing terror groups, have been dealt crushing blows by the Argentine military. And yet there had been no move towards a return to political normality. Close to 6,000 Argentines are believed still held without charge and each week the number of desaparecidos grows. The regime has spoken vaguely of returning the country to civilian rule by about 1991.

That date is uncertain because the military is first determined to erase the legend of Juan and Evita Perón before allowing Argentines the right to vote for their leaders. But despite the terror and murder of Perónista union officials, there is no sign of the legend fading. As senior officers have admitted, the slogan *'Puto o ladron, queremos a Perón'* (son of a bitch or thief, we love Perón) is still the unspoken thought of millions of Argentines. The generals tried once before — from 1955 to 1973 — to wean Argentina's working class people from their love of Perón. But when the dictator returned home, old and feeble, seven million Argentines voted for him to become their president again compared to two million who voted for his nearest rival. Asked before his death if he considered he had been a dictator, he laughed heartily and said: 'I consider dictator a pejorative word. There can be a dictator elected by the people. I was elected in two presidential elections by 60 to 70 percent of the popular vote.' Responding to charges of having been a demagogue, he said, 'And what do you call a politician who keeps his word?' As to accusations of having used brutality towards his opponents, he said, 'I never killed anybody. Nobody died with his shoes on.'

There is every reason to believe that when Argentines are once again given the chance to express their views at the ballot box they will vote for whoever they believe to be carrying the flag of Perón and Evita. Between them, they gave their descamisados a sense of self-respect and an appreciation of their importance to the nation. Of course, the economic benefits they gained then have long since disappeared. So has the power they wielded through the CGT. In fact, everything is as it was before. The country is ruled through a coalition of the military and the aristocracy just as it was until Colonel Perón's coup of 1943. The difference now is that working people in Argentina know they can win power whenever they are given the freedom of the secret ballot box. It will be then that they will make their comparisons.

In what they remember as the good old days, they used to fill the Plaza de Mayo to cheer their heroes with cries of 'Pay-ron! Pay-ron Ay-vita! Ay-vita!' as the Peróns appeared on the balcony of the palace to woo their descamisados. Now the only crowds that appear in the plaza are the mothers of the desaparecidos who gather by the hundreds every Thursday to exchange information and console each other. One week the sobbing was so loud that an embarrassed President Videla, who could hear the women from his office, ordered the police to disperse them. Scores were arrested. To the Argentines silent in their villa miserias, the slums on the edge of the city, the comparison is simple — between the present era of President Videla's desaparecidos and the era of the descamisados of Evita Perón.

184

BIBLIOGRAPHY

The fire that burned down my house in Los Angeles three years ago, destroying ten volumes of research material for this book as well as everything else I possessed, was the reason for the absence of both bibliography and footnotes in the previous edition of *Evita— First Lady*. I have been criticized for the lack of both. And I am concerned that I should have given credit to the authors whose books provided me with so much history and background as I put together my own story of Evita. Without my research material, it is impossible to provide adequate footnotes. But I have added an abridged bibliography to this new edition in the hope that the authors concerned will accept both my thanks and my apologies.

—J. B., 1980

Alexander, Robert J. *An Introduction to Argentina*. New York: Praeger, 1969.

Barager, Joseph R., ed. *Why Peron Came to Power: The Background to Peronism in Argentina*. New York: Knopf, 1968.

Bruce, James. *Those Perplexing Argentines*. New York: Longmans, Green, 1953.

Bunge, Alejandro. *Una Nueva Argentina*. Buenos Aires: Kraft, 1940.

Bunkley, Allison Williams. *The Life of Sarmiento*. New York: Greenwood, 1952.

Canal Frau, Salvador. *Las Poblaciones Indigenas de la Argentina*. Buenos Aires: Sudamericana, 1973.

Cooke, John William. *La Lucha por la Liberacion Nacional*. Buenos Aires: Granica Editor, 1971.

Cowles, Fleur. *Bloody Precedent*. New York: Random House, 1952.

Duarte, Erminda. *Mi hermana Evita*. Buenos Aires: Centro de estudios Eva Peron, 1972.

Ferns, H. S. *The Argentine Republic 1516–1971*. New York: Barnes & Noble Books, 1973.

Fotheringham, Ignacio H. *La Vida de un Soldado o Reminiscencias de la Fronteras*. Buenos Aires: Circulo Militar, 1970.

Franco, Juan Pablo, and Alvarez, Fernando. *Peronismo: Antecedentes y Gobierno*. Buenos Aires: Artex, 1972.

Goldwert, Marvin, *Democracy, Militarism and Nationalism in Argentina, 1930–1966: An Interpretation*. Latin American Monographs. Austin, Texas: University of Texas Press, 1972.

Greenup, Leonard and Ruth Robinson. *Revolution Before Breakfast: Argentina, 1941–1946*. Chapel Hill, N.C.: University of North Carolina Press, 1947.

Herring, Hubert. *A History of Latin America*. New York: Knopf, 1965.

Hirst, W. A. *Argentina*. New York: Scribner's, 1910.

Hudson, W. H. *Far Away and Long Ago*. Folcroft, Pa.: Folcroft, 1973.

Josephs, Ray. *Argentina Diary: The Inside Story of the Coming of Fascism*. New York: Random House, 1944.

Lanuza, Jose Luis. *The Gaucho*. New York: Crown.

Main, Mary Foster (Maria Flores). *The Woman with the Whip: Eva Peron*. Garden City, N.Y.: Doubleday, 1952.

Owen, Frank. *Peron, His Rise and Fall*. London, Cresset Press, 1957.

Pendle, George. *Argentina*. London: Oxford University Press, 1963.

Peron, Juan Domingo. *La Hora de los Pueblos*. Buenos Aires: Norte, 1968.

Rennie, Ysabel F. *The Argentine Republic*. New York: Macmillan, 1945.

Santander, Silvano. *Nazismo en Argentina*. Montevideo: Pueblos Unidos, 1945.

Scobie, James R. *Argentina: A City and a Nation*. New York, Oxford University Press, 1964.

Whitaker, Arthur P. *Argentina*. Englewood Cliffs, N.J.: Prentice-Hall, 1964.

White, John W. *Argentina: The Life Story of a Nation*. New York: Viking, 1942.

I have been collecting material on Argentina since I first went there to work for the *Buenos Aires Herald* in 1955, the year that Juan Peron was overthrown. My voluminous files, spanning many years, included stories from *The New York Times*, *The New York Herald Tribune*, *The Christian Science Monitor*, *Time*, *Newsweek*, *The Times* (London), *The Daily Telegraph*, and *The Guardian*. Sadly, all those treasured clips disappeared in the fire.

Index

Index

192

194

196